Singing

and the Etheric Tone

Singing

and the Etheric Tone

Gracia Ricardo's Approach to Singing,
based on her work with Rudolf Steiner

HILDA DEIGHTON and GINA PALERMO

Edited, with an Introduction and Afterword,

by DINA SORESI WINTER

✐ Anthroposophic Press

Published by Anthroposophic Press
RR 4, Box 94 A-1, Hudson, New York 12534

Copyright © 1991 Anthroposophic Press

Library of Congress Cataloging-in-Publication Data

Deighton, Hilda, 1890-1976
  Singing and the etheric tone : Gracia Ricardo's approach to singing, based
on her work with Rudolf Steiner / Hilda Deighton and Gina Palermo :
edited, with an introduction and afterword, by Dina Soresi Winter.
    p. cm.
  Includes bibliographical references.
  ISBN 0-88010-356-6
  1. Singing—Methods. 2. Ricardo, Gracia. I. Steiner, Rudolf, 1861-1925.
II. Palermo, Gina, d. 1963. III. Winter, Dina Soresi. IV. Title.
MT825.D35 1991
783-dc20   91-3655
                                                            CIP
                                                            MN

10 9 8 7 6 5 4 3 2 1

Printed in the United States of America

The editor and the publisher
gratefully dedicate this book to the memory of

MARY THEODORA RICHARDS
(November 6, 1908—November 20, 1990)

without whose devotion and determination
this work would never have come into print.

CONTENTS

FOREWORD

Until the beginning of the twentieth century, singing was a natural part of human life. Many aspects of everyday life were accompanied by general singing or songs actually connected with a specific activity—loggers' songs, railway workers' songs, household songs. The last echo of these could still be heard until World War II in children's songs. Only songs of religious life have enjoyed, within their church setting, an unbroken continuity.

Singing is a divine gift bestowed upon human beings. Through singing, a human being can create balance and harmony in the physical, soul, and spiritual aspects of life. This study by Hilda Deighton, Gina Palermo, Theodora Richards, and Dina Soresi Winter provides a helpful source for those who wish to gain a deeper understanding of singing and of the work of Gracia Ricardo. We see how Gracia Ricardo's lifelong devotion to the art of singing merged totally with her deep dedication to anthroposophy. The insights she gained from Rudolf Steiner personally, and from his books and lectures, placed her in a unique position both as a singer and as a pioneer within the Anthroposophical Society from the early years of the twentieth century until her death in 1955.

This work may thus serve as a tribute to a special individuality as well as a practical guide for those who wish to discover new dimensions in singing.

VIRGINIA SEASE
Dornach, Switzerland
December 1988

INTRODUCTION

A Spiritual Approach to Singing

Most modern training in singing is based upon methods which consider only the physical organism. Contemporary methods of voice production often include the showing of charts to students as part of the lesson—charts indicating the organs connected with singing (larynx, tongue, soft palate, hard palate, diaphragm). These charts are used to demonstrate what happens, or is supposed to happen, to the vocal organs as one sings. They are meant to be a conscious aid in learning how to sing better.

Despite these good intentions, I have known of several singers who initially had very good voices yet who emerged in complete desperation from these vocal studios, wondering if they would ever be able to sing again. Because they could not squeeze themselves into the fixed forms demanded of them by their teachers, they fled. Some sought their own paths and found the key which led them to their own individual singing freedom. Birgit Nilsson, the great Swedish soprano, was one who did. But not many can do so. Consequently, it often happens that singers who have been through a full university training which includes such a mechanical approach can hardly produce a joyful tone again. Their singing is tight, unfree, and certainly not a healing experience for themselves or for their listeners. It would have been far better for these singers if they had not undertaken voice training at all! This is not to imply that there are not good singing teachers in the universities and in private studios. There are, although it is not a common occurrence to find them. There are certainly gifted teachers who know a great deal about the voice, who still have an intuitive, innate feeling for good singing, and know how to use imaginative pictures and a fine sense of hearing to guide their gifted pupils to a healthy sound.

Those who are considered the best teachers, however, will usually be unwilling to work with singers who have "no voice," meaning no voice for a professional career. But what about all those who might wish to study voice for their own self-development, for the joy and well-being of singing; who sense the importance of singing well, both for themselves and for the sake of bringing a freer, more joyful tone to their singing in community? Singing, after all, is the birthright of every human being, the expression of our humanity. "If more people would sing," Rudolf Steiner once said, "there would be less crime in the world." What would he have said today? We know that in our schools—especially our public schools—singing, along with the other arts, is often the first to be eliminated from the curriculum: when budgetary problems demand cuts, the arts are the first to go. Yet, if we wish to cultivate humanity in our children, in addition to making them smart and successful in the so-called "hard world of reality," then we need to give them what will help them stand in the world as whole, balanced adults. The arts can help here, but they must be truly artistic, not just "arty." There must be knowledge and depth to them. Rudolf Steiner, for example, recognized the importance both of including the arts in a child's education and of an artistic approach to all the subjects, as may be seen in the curriculum of the Waldorf Schools throughout the world. He recognized that singing is an aspect of the human being that should not, must not, be neglected. "Music is there to make us human." And of all the instruments available to us, singing is the most direct means of human expression. Singing, which is available to everyone, connects us with our divine, spiritual origins, with the truly human in ourselves and in each other. We need more of it, not less. To sing together as adults, with and for our children in a healthy and joyful way, is essential in the struggle to stay human. We cannot teach our children how to sing with formal singing lessons. They can only imitate what we hope will be a free and joyful sound. We must be able to lead them with our own free singing. For this, only an approach that recognizes soul and spiritual dimensions in the human being can be helpful. Methods based on physiology alone can only hinder the free expression of song.

In most of the accepted methods of teaching singing today, however, the prevailing concern is how the physical organs can be manipulated and controlled to produce tones. Only the very gifted singer knows instinctively how to avoid the pitfall of singing too mechanically. The artist in them often discovers a more spiritual awareness of singing and so avoids the tendency to get stuck in an approach that is purely physical. But, as such instincts forsake us more and more, we may well ask: What will the future have in store for singing and its representatives?

Gracia Ricardo asked this very question of Rudolf Steiner in the early years of this century. He answered that singing is not a physical process. He said that singing must be freed from a mechanical approach and the singer awakened to an understanding of *true tone*, to an appreciation of tone as a spiritual reality. When this happens the singer can experience what Rudolf Steiner referred to as the "leading over of the tone into the etheric." And then a new approach to singing may arise wherein the singer will have the all-engrossing experience of his whole being as a "resounding column of tone." The entire etheric organization of the human being—all of his life forces—then becomes involved in the singing process. One's whole being sings. Great singers have had this experience. Now the path to it must become conscious for all. Not that we can all become professional singers, but we can all learn how to sing well. This is one way to help us find our humanity.

The Method and How It Came About

Gracia Ricardo was a professional singer. Early in her studies and while still a young girl she lost the use of her voice through vocal strain and an illness that kept her bedridden for several months. As her strength gradually returned she developed, while lying on her back, an approach to singing that returned the use of her voice. The new approach was the kernel of a singing method that would later take shape, form, and substance through her ever-deepening connection with anthroposophy and her numerous conversations with Rudolf Steiner. "You have the free tone," Rudolf Steiner would often tell her when she questioned him about her method of singing. Once, when faced with a concert in Los Angeles in a huge theater with a sixty-piece orchestra, she feared her voice might not carry. "Shall I alter my approach for this concert?" she cabled Steiner. Again he answered: "Alter nothing. You have the free tone."

Gracia Ricardo became part of an intimate circle of pupils surrounding Rudolf Steiner in the early years of anthroposophy. Encouraged by Steiner, and on the basis of her conversations with him, and through her study of the many references to singing, eurythmy, and music in his writings, Gracia Ricardo evolved a new art of singing, an art that leads the singer to a real experience of the etheric activity in singing. Instead of beginning with physical functions, she started with the *tone* itself, which she understood as being based on the *word*. This word is best begun with the help of a consonant, which gives the tone an acoustical shell. Within this shell, all resonators can freely resound, thus revealing the full capacity of the voice.

The cultivation of a sense of hearing is an important part of this approach to singing. Tone is carried through the air to our ears, but it is the *etheric* which carries the real essence of the tone to our inner being. An intensified listening carries the outer tone within; and the subsequent inner experience greatly affects the tone that can then be sung. Goethe once wrote in his *Tonlehre* (*Theory of Tone*):

> One should pay particular attention to the leading of the tone inward through the ear, which acts in a thoroughly stimulating and productive way on the voice. The activity of the voice is thereby awakened, set in motion, enhanced, and increased. The whole body is activated.

Besides the development of an inner sense of hearing—which carries the outer tone within—the attainment of the etheric tone in singing requires that we as singers find a path that allows us to bring our own true tone to birth. To develop the voice in a more conscious and healthy way that includes the spiritual dimension of the human being, we need to find a means whereby the tone we sing can reflect the universal tone that streams around us. When we link ourselves to this tone in the right way, it flows and resounds through us.

Theodora Richards, who studied with her aunt Gracia Ricardo for many years, maintained that the concept of the "embouchure" is essential to this approach. She referred to this "embouchure" (a concept used by wind instrumentalists) as the proper starting point of the tone and as the focal point for singing. Imagine a point on the lower lip, where the inner air meets the outer; imagine that the tone starts right there. Imagine that the tone comes as much from without as from within: where it meets is the embouchure, the imaginary point where, when we sing, the tone first comes to birth.

The tone referred to here is of course the tone as it sounds in the world. That tone comes toward the singer from without, and is met by a tone from within. This tone, that comes from within the human being, according to indications of Rudolf Steiner, has its place of origin at the pineal gland. Other singing methods, such as the Werbeck Method, are founded on this insight. The two approaches are by no means contradictory. In truth, it is the combination of ear, pineal gland, and embouchure which, together with what comes from without, creates the birth of the sounding tone.

The embouchure must be employed in a comfortable range of the voice. There must be no vocal strain. (Teacher demonstration is essential at the beginning of the Ricardo method.) If this anchor for the voice, the embouchure, is properly found, as the voice soars upward or downward, the tones find their own placement —their own proper home in and around us. The body becomes the firm yet flexible instrument which gives the proper physical basis for each emerging tone. Our task as singers is then to consciously *allow* the necessary processes to take place so that the tones can be born through us in a free and healthy way. The whole body is activated from above the head to below the feet, so to speak, not in a state of tautness, but in a state of balance between relaxation and proper tension. The state is one of awake readiness. Like one listening for a distant sound in the dark, the singer must find his inner and outer balance on each tone and each tone must find its own balance in the singer.

Each rise or fall of the voice needs a new set of subtle inner adjustments, which the singer cannot possibly control in a purely physical way, any more than an archer can control each minor adjustment of arm and hand when drawing the bow to shoot an arrow. But the archer can keep his eyes on the goal and see to it that no rigidities prevent the taking of good aim. The *ear* is for the singer, what the *eye* is for the archer.

With the embouchure, we have a means of leading the tone into that etheric realm of which Rudolf Steiner speaks. Moreover, the embouchure provides the proper start of the tone by means of a word correctly enunciated on a given pitch. Once the tone is "there" in an unforced but definite way, the other tones can follow on the same stream and the organism

18

experiences a balanced inner mobility. This process, of course, must include a flexible action of the diaphragm based on proper breathing. A healthy stream of sound for the entire range of the voice can thus be achieved. In singing, there is movement: not just an outpouring of sound, but a balanced inner and outer streaming of tones involving the whole organism and connecting us with the universal tone. The process of singing is a receiving as well as a giving.

Lamperti, the celebrated Italian vocal master of the nineteenth century, had a sense for this receptive aspect of singing when he spoke of "drinking in the tone" (*"bere il suono"*). We activate this universal tone within us when we sing correctly. It is as if beings were weaving in, out, and around us in flowing movement as we sing. Indeed, Elizabeth Rethberg, the great Metropolitan Opera singer, once confided to Franz Winkler that she always knew when she was singing correctly: When the singing was right, she saw spiritual beings in movement around her. When the singing was not right, they were not there. By this, she knew whether she was achieving her true goal, irrespective of the audience's enthusiastic applause.

In her essay "The Singer as Instrument," Theodora Richards writes:

> Those who wish to link their song with the tone streaming through the world around them cannot remain just as they are. They must lift their mood to another level and cultivate receptive quiet and attentive listening. These qualities are basic to becoming an instrument for the world of tone to play upon. The sound each species of animal instinctively makes has its own distinctive tonal timbre. This allows only a partial inflowing of the universal tone. Tones may be conjured forth from all sorts of inanimate objects. But a human being must deliberately undergo a spiritual discipline to become, with his own unique timbre, a fuller,

19

more complete and individualized instrument of this universal tone.

This is what my aunt and teacher Grace Richards [Gracia Ricardo] did. Prompted by her study of anthroposophy and her personal conversations with Rudolf Steiner, she developed a new method of "etheric" singing.... This training starts with the cultivation of the right mood. First of all, one must find the calm to enter into a new dimension of reverent receptivity in order to experience the universal tone. Grace Richards used the phrase, *Erwartungsvolle Ruhe*—"Expectant calm." "Try not to try," she often said. The over-intensity that accompanies "trying hard" sets up tensions in the vocal instrument that block the free flowing of the tone. Naturally, the physical body, as the singer's instrument, must be accorded due consideration. To enhance relaxation, a student could begin a practice session in a sitting position, comfortably erect, and do a few deep breathing exercises. An exacting ear training is of the essence. This should lead to the ability to hear with accuracy and discrimination the nuances of the teacher's illustrations, as well as to judge properly one's own attempts. A teacher's vocal illustrations are indispensable for teaching this method. Unlike other methods, in which the tone production comes first, and the speech sound follows, the pupil is asked instead to concentrate upon the initial consonant which, properly centered, provides the "house," the shape within which the vowel is intoned on the desired pitch.

The centering or focusing of the tone is achieved through an articulated embouchure. A flautist finds an embouchure essential—so likewise a singer. This is by far the most unique and vital aspect of the method. One trains this embouchure by means of pictures.

Visualize a tiny spot or aperture, localized at the

midpoint of the lower lip. Upon this imaginary pinpoint, the word is spoken in an unforced manner, centered and concentrated.... The breath in the singer's mouth comes in contact with the outside air around the lips. The outside air, molded by the properly formed, articulated speech sound, acts like a sounding board or acoustical shell for all the resonators of head, nose, chest, mouth, and so forth; in short, of the entire vocal instrument, thereby giving the voice a free, full, ringing quality. The vibration thus set in motion comes about through the interplay of the universal tone and the singer, not by a forced physical effort.... The inside and outside air then maintain a balanced interchange through the embouchure. This balance is called the focus, and is the seed-center which produces the freely floating, round, ringing etheric tone....

A focused word on the desired pitch is thus the crux of this method... and its lofty goal is the marrying of speech and tone—needless to say, a lifetime study.

We can be grateful to Theodora Richards for introducing us to Gracia Ricardo's comprehensive and rich view of singing. Richards' own significant contribution was in the developing of the understanding of this helpful technique of using the embouchure. Italian teachers of voice would refer to singing "on the lips" ("*sulle labra*") or "forward" ("*davanti*"). Singing forward is not to be understood in any way as pushing or forcing the tone outward, which could only be detrimental to the voice and to good singing. Theodora Richards' explanation of the embouchure makes understandable the orginal meaning of this term in a way that is clear and usable for us today.

Gina Palermo and Hilda Deighton met Gracia Ricardo in New York City in the early 1920s. Through that meeting Gina Palermo and Hilda Deighton, already professional singers, both became Gracia Ricardo's pupils and lifelong friends. They recognized what Ricardo—a devoted student of Rudolf Steiner and of anthroposophy—could offer them: a new dimension in singing, a practical training with a spiritual dimension and foundation, and a conscious understanding of what they were doing when they were singing well. For over twenty years they studied with Gracia Ricardo, following her back and forth from New York to Switzerland, diligently recording the results of their study. Gradually, a manuscript containing an exposition of the Ricardo method took shape. This was a life's work. They worked on it together until Gina's death in 1963. Hilda carried on and indeed was still working on it a few weeks before her death in 1976. The task then fell to Theodora Richards to bring this work to fruition. But much effort was still needed to organize and coordinate it into book form and my enthusiasm for the substance of the work led Theodora to ask my help in preparing it for publication. *Singing and the Etheric Tone* is thus the priceless legacy not only of Gina Palermo and Hilda Deighton's devotion to the art of singing and to their teacher's unique anthroposophical method, but also of Theodora Richards' loyal and tenacious will to see it in print.

Singing and the Etheric Tone presents a few indicators along the way toward freer and more joyful singing. It is not, however, meant to be a "do-it-yourself" manual, for no one can learn to sing from a book. But the open-minded singer who has already achieved a degree of freedom and good technique will be able to recognize and make use of sound vocal ideas and may find that this offering promotes a more conscious, and safer, approach to singing.

No one method or approach to singing should be regarded as the only one. Gracia Ricardo herself was the first to admit that her approach should be regarded as but one of the ways by which to achieve freedom in singing based upon the spiritual scientific principles given by Rudolf Steiner. Every healthy, sound approach to singing will find meeting points with other

22

approaches to singing. The dimension which is new here is the spiritual-scientific view of anthroposophy. On this basis, the old can be understood in a new way, and a conscious approach, more appropriate to our day, can become the basis for a new school of singing that does not in any way ignore or minimize the wisdom of the past but, in fact, still draws fully upon it.

Singing, we open ourselves to those forces that lift us above the everyday world. When we sing together, we meet each other on a deeper level than usual. Rightly experienced, singing links us with the etheric realm, with each other, and with the spiritual source of tone itself.

DINA SORESI WINTER
1991

CHAPTER ONE

The Onset of the Tone (The Attack)

With the onset or start of the tone, sometimes called the "attack," the word (the clear vowel and consonant sound) is of primary importance, for it is the position and the correct form of the *word* that determine the freedom and beauty of the *tone*.

In singing, a student needs the help of imaginative pictures. Just as the horn player must acquire the embouchure in order to play his instrument, so must the singer find the point of contact for the start of the tone. The tone is a spiritual reality, which comes as much from outside, toward the singer, as from within. The point of contact is an imaginary point where outside and inside tone meet. This is the singer's embouchure. The horn player must gain control of the muscles of his lips, but the singer must not consciously call these muscles into action. As one speaks the vowel on a pitch, the life forces (etheric forces) activate the (physical) muscles and set them in motion. The impulse to sing does not originate in the muscles; rather, the muscles follow the impulse.

The Focus of the Tone

The mental picture of a tiny spot or aperture on the middle of the lower lip must rise before the singer, and the word is to be intoned upon this imaginary pinpoint. (It must be understood that we are referring here primarily to the middle and lower range of the voice and not to the higher tones which require a different placement.) The word must be small and highly concentrated, as it cannot *grow* if it is too large in the beginning. Every vowel must be spoken into the imaginary "dome of the consonant." For instance, in singing the word "bode," the "b" is the consonant into which the "o" is sounded; or, in the word "see," "s" is the consonant into which you pour the "ee." The "ee" form has a natural focusing quality. Therefore all the vowels must contain the thought of "ee," so that the focusing resonance in "ee" may become the center point and kernel of every vowel.

This "ee" resonance lifts the voice out of heaviness, giving it a quality of light. The "ee" should live in every word that is sung and rise into the resonators of the head. But this "resonating ee," which resonates through all the vowels, should not be confused with the simple vowel "e." The simple "e" vowel should, of course, also contain the "ee" resonance.

The Humming Approach

In some singing methods, pupils are taught to precede the starting of a tone with a slight humming sound in the nose. This amounts to starting the tone by trying to sing the consonant "m," instead of a vowel, and is directly at variance with the approach we are describing. Humming is the consonant "m" prolonged. It closes the lips and draws the sound into the nasal cavities. It is sometimes considered helpful in relieving tension in the throat, but when "m" is used in this way the teacher is correcting one vocal fault by replacing it with another. The resonance, which some seek through humming, must be attained not by activating the resonating cavities of the head with the "m" consonant, but by coming to an understanding of the natural focusing resonance of the vowel "e" in every intoned word. It is impossible to sing a tone on a consonant. The singer can produce no musical tone except through the medium of a vowel. Though many teachers believe that humming helps to focus the voice, the effort of consciously directing the voice through the "m" sound can be a cause of strain. Tone is not a material substance and it cannot be put or placed anywhere. It is not mere sound, which can be measured according to its vibrations. In his course of lectures on "Light," Rudolf Steiner made a statement that was not intended particularly for singers but that is of great significance for them:

> Just as the light is not a result of mechanical vibrations, but a form of existence or being, so also is tone something that exists of itself, not something that arises out of mechanical vibrations.
>
> Rudolf Steiner, *Light Course*

Once the tone is there, it can be measured, but the mechanical vibrations are not the source of the tone. Here one can truly say that the whole is more than the sum of its parts.

Separation of Word and Tone

When the word is merely sung out on the breath stream, the result is a mixture of tone and word, but if one keeps in mind the need for a conscious control of the intoned word or embouchure, and if the word is intoned on the lips without anticipation of the tone which is to follow, immediate separation of word and tone takes place. The separation is only momentary, but tonal purity depends upon it. The vowel is intoned on the contact point, finished, and allowed instantly to *become* tone, which rises of its own accord into the head resonators. If this separation does not take place, tone and word can get caught in the mouth, producing a cavernous, muffled, or mouthy sound.

Listening for the Word

Many singers make the mistake of listening to their own voices, from a purely tonal standpoint, without taking much notice of the vowels they are singing. Students must be awakened to the importance of the vowel; their attention must be directed toward it. The clarity and form of the vowel are of primary importance.

The vowel is the part of the word that creates the tone. It should be demonstrated to students that the final instant of the vowel is *breath*, controlled by the imaginary embouchure, not physically by the lips. The embouchure is the etheric form, which is the preparation for the birth of the tone. There should be no stiffening of the upper lip to finish the pronunciation of the word. Stiffening the upper lip lifts the word out of its proper position at the very last second, spoiling the beauty of the tone. The final consonant, swiftly and carefully pronounced, must finish the word—and this consonant should be pronounced at the last possible moment. The singer sings vowels, not consonants. Once the consonant is pronounced, the tone is finished. The illustration shows a simple exercise:

It is the "ee" in "kee" that is sung. "K" is the consonant form into which the vowel "ee" is poured. Speak the "ee" into the imaginary form of the consonant "k" and sustain it over the five notes, slowly, finishing the word with "p," which should be pronounced swiftly, but not sung.

The Starting Point to which the Vowel Returns

In the preceding exercise, the "ee" begins on the note G and uses this G pitch as a pivot. The singer can now move the vowel in all directions, and for any distance, up and down the scale, but its central point, the kernel of concentration, remains where it was at the start of the tone. The starting point of the pitch G is the vowel's home and to this it must return. The notes A and F#, which occur in the exercise, should not be regarded as new and different notes, each requiring a separate start, but as part of the original start of the tone. In this exercise, the word or vowel is spoken *once*, not repeated anew on each note.

Muscular Interference

In singing, one does not project or push out the word or vowel, but merely *pronounces* it. We must keep remembering that the word comes as much from outside the mouth as from inside. The word, which comes toward us from the cosmos, is picked up by the singer from the space outside. At the moment of contact, the word is born to human experience. In pronouncing it, the singer should not prolong or hold on to it in an effort to control it, but should finish it immediately, returning in imagination to the point of contact as explained above. This must be done within a split second, for it is during this instant that the word becomes tone, and rises into the resonating cavities of the head. At this crucial moment one is tempted to add something of one's own, some assistance, but any help the singer could give would be muscular, and this should be avoided.

It is natural for the singer producing the tone to feel that something must done to help it along—but the singer must do *nothing*. The famous singing teacher Herbert Wilber Greene writes in his book *The Singer's Ladder*, "Keep trying not to try." This was also a Ricardo maxim.

Proper Conception of Vowels and Consonants

In speech, as used by an actor or a speech therapist, for instance, the vowels and consonants can be formed consciously at various places within the mouth. This can never be the case in singing. For the singer, as for the speaker, the physical tools of enunciation are the tongue, the teeth, the palate, and the lips. However, it must be clear that the *conception* of the vowels and consonants is what causes them to be formed at different places in the mouth. Of course, when one sings or speaks, a physical action takes place in the larynx (the drawing together of the vocal cords), but the action of the larynx is the result and not the cause of the sound. The singer does not bring the vocal cords together by a conscious act of will. We sing and the rest follows. The correctly pronounced and sung word brings the proper muscles into play. Impure vowels in singing are like muddy colors in painting. One can create nothing beautiful with them. Singing is the word further ennobled by tone. A proper conception of the vowels and consonants *molds the vocal organs.*

The Consonant Form and the Vowel

The light that lives within the vowel shines,
enclosed, protected, cherished, held in place
by many-sided care of consonants.

Albert Steffen ("The Mercury Capital")

The imagination of the consonant form must arise simultaneously with the enunciation of a vowel or word. The "consonant form" used in this singing method does not have a physical reality. It is, however, spiritually real, and the student must learn to grasp its spiritual reality. To most students who are unacquainted with the background of Gracia Ricardo's method of producing vocal tone, the consonant form is referred to simply as "an imaginative picture"—like, for instance, the "dome" of a consonant, a vaulted dome in which there is space for the vowel to live.

If the word is intoned without keeping the "form" in mind, one produces a comparatively colorless tone, often lacking in overtones. In order to attain color and provide space, one must always think the form. One should not, however, think the form *before* intoning the word, as this results in a wrapping up of both word and tone and creates a muffled sound. If the word is not surrounded by a form, the resulting tone may dissipate. The breath will stream out around it, unused and wasted, and the tone will be diffused and possess no central point or kernel of concentration.

The concept of an etheric form is an etheric imagination. The form should not be conceived of as merely a shell or dome. It is living and limitless. It may be pictured as being as large as the cosmic dome. Indeed, it is the image of this vast form that gives

31

the voice a free and limitless quality. At first, the student is asked to think of the form as surrounding the head, more to the front than to the back, and it is into this imaginary, malleable, living "house"—this inverted chalice—that the vowel or word is spoken. Later, when the student has mastered the method, the consonant form becomes the great limitless space into which the song is poured. The concept of perfect, intoned speech within this etheric form is too profound to be fully grasped intellectually by the brain. Only when the spiritual ear or inner hearing sense is trained can one gradually come to know whether or not one is proceeding correctly. A spiritualized inner hearing indicates whether or not one is singing etherically.

The Supporting Breath

Having created the embouchure (the etheric point between the outside and the inside word) and produced a tone, how do we support it? Do we need to do deep-breathing exercises and develop our muscles, or learn to hold our breath to a stop watch?

Many people think so, and at every gathering of singing teachers the subject is brought up for discussion. At such meetings, students of Gracia Ricardo's method usually stand alone. We do not think these conscious physical exercises are necessary. When Rudolf Steiner was asked, "What about breathing?" he answered wryly, "You breathe." Later, in 1920, speaking of the art of recitation, he said the following:

> What is at stake is not how the voice or tone can be sustained by some sort of external method of manipulating the breath or placing the voice, in the way taught by some bad singing teachers. The essential thing is that what should stay in the unconscious must still remain there when we are learning a subject such as this—a

person should not be wrenched out of everything unconscious through a clumsy treatment of the body. Rather, through proper artistic formation and artistic treatment we can train our breathing so that the whole process remains in a certain sphere of the unconscious, and yet is drawn up into the soul element which gives it artistic expression.

Rudolf Steiner, *Poetry and the Art of Speech*
(Lecture, October 13, 1920)

In many singing methods deep breathing exercises are an integral part of the training. The muscles around the diaphragm are developed like those of an athlete. Holding the breath for longer and longer periods of time is said to develop the lungs. Simple deep breathing is certainly beneficial to the general health, but such exercises, when used to prepare one for singing, are sometimes carried to lengths too ludicrous for serious consideration. All this physical development is said to be necessary to produce a tone and to support it. Instead of breathing exercises, however, the student should be taught the deeper aspects of breathing. Breathing is not merely a physical process. Through breathing, spiritual beings enter us and work in us. "In the human being," Rudolf Steiner pointed out:

material processes are continually occurring that are really spiritual processes. We breathe. And in breathing we take in oxygen. Not only do we take in oxygen but, since our breathing process is ruled by the same processes as the atmosphere in the outer world, we are subject to the rhythm of the whole universe. Thus, through the rhythmical processes we undergo in our organism, we also stand in a certain relationship to the environment. We do not merely breathe in oxygen, for something spiritual lives in the oxygenized breath. Material processes are the expression of spiritual processes.

Rudolf Steiner, *Folk Souls and the Mystery of Golgotha*
(Lecture, March 30, 1918)

When we inhale, we take in the creative formative forces of the cosmos—these forces are born again in us as we breathe. The process affects both the nervous system and the blood, and connects the physical organs with the spiritual world. Breathing is a grace given to us from the cosmos. It is the breath of life.

Singers must be taught to understand not only inhalation but exhalation as well, because exhalation is what concerns the singer most. Everyone has seen a singer gasping for breath or hurrying the phrase to get through it before the supply of breath gives out. No amount of inhalation will help, because the *exhalation* is at fault. As for inhalation, the lungs must be filled in a normal manner by taking a deep breath before singing. The chest should be held high, but relaxed. A feeling of expansion in the whole upper body will follow. In inhalation, the muscles of the back are brought into play to allow the lower ribs to expand. One can picture the lower ribs expanding outward like wings. This is a result of proper inhalation. The back muscles are not ordinarily used in everyday breathing, but singers call upon them every time they take a deep breath. The lungs need never be completely refilled at the end of a phrase, because they are never completely emptied. The breath must be replenished when necessary by silent, natural inhalation (through both nose and mouth), which will be felt in the lowest portion of the lungs. There will then always be a reserve supply of breath, which gives confidence not only to the singer but to the audience as well. Just as singers should have at their command at least one note higher than they will ever be expected to sing in public, so should they finish each phrase with enough extra breath to carry them through an additional measure should the need arise.

How is the breath supply correctly used? As the word is

intoned on the imaginary contact point on the lower lip, the breath is released by *controlled exhalation,* using only the amount needed to sustain and develop the tone. The word plays on the top of the breath stream like a ball on a jet of water—too little support and the ball sinks, too much and it is forced off. The tone is supported by the breath as a person is supported by the floor beneath the feet. The floor is not the person, and the breath is not the tone, but merely the supporter of the tone. Rudolf Steiner said:

Picture the tone here on earth, even the tone that reveals itself as sound: on earth it lives in the air. The scientific concept, however, is that the vibration of the air *is* the tone. This is a naive concept indeed. Imagine that here is the ground and that someone stands on it. Surely the ground is not the person, but it must be there so that the person can stand on it; otherwise he could not be there. You would not want to understand a human being, however, by the ground he stands on. Likewise, tone needs air for support. Just as a person stands on the firm ground—in a somewhat more complicated way—tone has its ground, its resistance, in the air. Air has no more significance for tone than the ground for the person who stands on it. Tone rushes toward air, and the air makes it possible for tone to 'stand'. Tone itself, however, is something spiritual. Just as the human being is different from the earthly ground on which he stands, so tone differs from the air on which it rises. Naturally it rises in complicated ways, in manifold ways. On earth, we can speak and sing only by means of air, and in the air formations of the tone element we have an earthly reflection of a soul-spiritual element. This soul-spiritual element of tone belongs in reality to the supersensible world. And what lives here in the air is basically the body of tone.

Rudolf Steiner, *The Inner Nature of Music and the Nature of Tone,* (Lecture IV, December 2, 1922)

The Diaphragm

The diaphragm is the breath muscle. It divides and, in a way, unites the metabolic and rhythmic systems—the will and feeling natures of the human being—and is the source of support for the breath. In the act of breathing the lungs are almost passive. The air flows in and out. The lungs are filled and then emptied.

It is the diaphragm which moves the air in and around us. The muscle of the diaphragm lies across the base of the lungs in the form of an arch. When one inhales, the muscle is contracted and the arch is flattened, thereby allowing the lungs to expand downward and to fill with air. The contracted diaphragm of the singer is charged with dynamic power and it is this strength, this intensity, of the diaphragm, and not merely the greater amount of breath, which supports the balanced flow of tone. Word and tone perfectly poised on the breath bring about breath control.

An increase in the amount of breath can be brought about through activities other than singing (in gymnastics for example), but the intensity in the diaphragm needed for singing can be achieved only when the diaphragm is supporting the rise and fall of tone. This is an activity of waking, day consciousness. Even the unconscious, sleeping human being inhales sufficient breath for the body's needs, but the active intensity of the diaphragm occurs only when the higher, "I" forces of the singer are consciously engaged in the act of singing. It is this intensity of the diaphragm, breathing intensified by artistic activity, that largely controls exhalation. Singing is a transformation of energy and breath into tone.

Again, the support of the diaphragm is much more than a purely physical activity. Controlling the muscle physically, and thereby supporting the tone by bodily means, will defeat us in our search for an etheric tone supported by the vital forces in the singer. Success depends upon vitality, in other words, upon our being filled with life. When vitality is low, the etheric forces are weaker. When vitality is high, the tone can be supported by the stronger etheric forces. In order to acquire intensity of the diaphragm, etheric forces, life forces, must be called into play. An etheric tone is a tone supported by the control of the life forces of the diaphragm. It is this etheric control which sustains a vitalized stream of breath.

Release

The obvious way to *end* a tone is to arrest the flow of breath supporting it. This can be done in three ways:

1. By momentarily stopping the breath stream supported by the diaphragm.

2. By contracting the muscles of the throat.

3. By closing the mouth.

The first is correct and results merely in a cessation of tone. The second creates an explosive sound of air in the throat. The third causes the consonants "m" or "p" to be heard at every release. Release is merely a cessation of sound. It is not a voluntary muscular action. The throat should remain open. To stop a tone, one simply withdraws the support of the vibrating breath column. If the natural coordinations in singing are operating freely and flexibly, however, one may experience an elastic, muscular reaction in the area of the diaphragm at the ending of a tone.

CHAPTER TWO

Classification of the Voice

The total range of the human voice from the lowest note of the bass singer to the highest tone of the soprano voice is a little over five octaves, from 55 to 1760 vibrations per second. This range has two main divisions, which overlap:

1. A range for male voices consisting of about three and one-half octaves from A to F#.

2. A range for female voices consisting of about three and one-half octaves from D to A#.

Male voices are classified as bass, baritone, and tenor; female voices as contralto, mezzo-soprano, and soprano. Subdivisions of these classifications (basso-profondo, bass-baritone, heroic tenor, lyric tenor, dramatic soprano, lyric soprano, coloratura soprano) are used to describe various qualities and characteristics inherent in the natural voice. The well-trained voice in any of these categories covers a span of two or two and one-half octaves.

The range alone does not determine the classification of the voice. In the final analysis, the quality of the voice determines its classification. If a male voice boasts a fine, resounding low G, one can assume it is a bass, but it is not always easy to distinguish a baritone from a potential tenor. Many celebrated tenors began their public careers as baritones.

The situation is the same for female voices. If a young girl can display a natural, unforced high C she is a soprano, but whether the voice will extend into the octave above and develop the flexibility necessary for a coloratura soprano, or display the pure and limpid quality of the lyric soprano, or mature into the rich timbre and deep range of the dramatic soprano—is a question only time and training can answer. Many dramatic sopranos sing lower in the scale than contraltos, and their low notes are just as rich, but the quality of their middle and upper voice is different from that of the contralto. Contraltos sometimes blossom into dramatic sopranos. *The voice, when liberated from physical interference, goes to its natural home.*

Imitation

Strange as it may seem, some of the best singing teachers of the past were themselves unable to sing. When presenting the concepts indicated in this book, the teacher should be able to illustrate with his or her own voice the points raised in each lesson.

The teacher must be alert, however, to the pupil's tendency to imitate the quality of his or her voice and this should be discouraged. What the teacher does may be imitated, but the *quality* of the teacher's voice should not be heard in the voice of the pupil. Each voice is unique and is a reflection of the inner being. Socrates said: "Let me hear his voice that I may know him." Every voice differs from all others, and its individual beauty should be brought out by good training.

The teacher's task is to recognize where the pupil's voice belongs and to bring out all of its latent qualities within the limits of its natural, unforced scope.

Extending the Range

In extending the range of the voice, beginning exercises should be limited to the part of the scale produced with the greatest ease. This is usually the section lying in or near the range of the natural speaking voice because here a true relation to the speaking voice can be established. The student is given vocal exercises that guide him toward a perfect start of the tone. Under the teacher's supervision, sustained tones are sung which bring breath control to the fore, and ideas about resonance are then presented. Exercises in the extreme high range, where strain might be felt, are avoided. A middle-range song is assigned, allowing the student to apply immediately what he has learned.

In the age of Bel Canto, when the voice was trained as a musical instrument, the student was kept for a year or more on a page of exercises. This method does not make sense for our time. Songs bring up various vocal problems which can be pointed out, discussed, and overcome. When a song presents a problem, the teacher will develop an exercise to meet the difficulty. The late Isadore Luckstone, famous New York singing teacher, said:

A great variety of exercises can be found in wisely selected songs. If exercises can be thought of as phrases of a song, they will become vehicles of expressive meaning instead of lifeless vocalisers.

"A Vocal Presentation" (An Interview),
Etude, Philadelphia, 1941

The "song approach" has many advocates who believe the pupil gains more by working at practical problems than by the exclusive study of technicalities. A song is less abstract than an exercise, and while learning, the student's imagination is stimulated by work on songs which do not exceed his capabilities. The scales are taught by concealing them within melodious exercises resembling songs and arias, where the flow of the song carries the voice along, rhythmically and effortlessly.

The practice of the "great scale," sometimes called the "slow scale"[1] is invaluable to the mature singer but is discouraged for beginners as it may produce tension. Practice should be done with a medium amount of tone, neither too loud nor too soft, and home practice should at first be limited to ten-minute periods twice a day.

Some teachers train the middle voice tone by tone, adding new notes one at a time to the top or bottom, thus extending the scale from the middle in both directions. This is usually

---

[1]The "great scale," devised by Lilli Lehmann, the noted Metropolitan Opera singer, goes up very slowly from one tone to the next for one octave at a time (for example, from low C to middle C, from low D to middle D, etc.) and then returns down the scale to the original note. Lehmann's book *How to Sing* gives details.

done by working on a slow scale, but we prefer introducing the new notes by means of the broken arpeggio, beginning in a low key and working up as far as the voice will easily go.

The first three notes are sung staccato, rhythmically, with plenty of time in between, and the highest note should be sung as a *passing* note with no expectation of holding it. It is much easier to take a high note in passing than to sustain it. If the singer continues to practice by singing the highest note as a passing note without preparing to hold it, she will eventually be able to sing her highest notes without effort. The exercise should be used in all parts of the voice, as low and as high as the singer can easily sing. Slowly but surely, the range will extend.

The Gift

When Rossini was asked, "What is the chief requirement for a singer?" he answered, "Voice." But Rossini was not a singing teacher! If he had been, he would have given the question deeper thought. There have been great and famous singers whose art far outstripped their vocal gifts, and there have been those whose beautiful voices were not gifts at all, but the fruit of painstaking cultivation. A fine natural voice is certainly a great asset and sometimes makes the path to success shorter, but in some cases it has even proved to be a handicap. What nature has bestowed so generously upon a singer makes hard work seem unnecessary, and the singer's art fails to grow and mature. The singer remains a gifted vocalist who has not learned how to sing, for the art of singing is seldom a natural gift and must be pursued for its own sake. A good voice is not synonymous with good singing. The less gifted pupil with a feeling of dedication to the art can sometimes go much further than one with a glorious natural voice and less will.

Building a Voice

A young student who wishes to learn to play the piano or the violin can begin by purchasing a good instrument in perfect condition. This is not the case with the student of singing. The raw material which the pupil brings to the teacher is often of inferior quality, and an adequate instrument must first be made of it before the pupil can become a singer.

Sometimes the student with a mediocre voice has a great longing to sing. Perhaps this student possesses many of the other requisites such as good health, a fine ear, open-mindedness, tonal imagination, artistic discrimination, and the ability to accept and assimilate instruction. Such students often tell the teacher they do not hope for a career, but wish to study solely for their own pleasure. The first lesson can open up a new world to them. Gradually tone becomes an important part of life and a rich realm of poetry unfolds as they study the great vocal literature. Frequently the seemingly inconsequential voice begins to gain color and resonance and expands beyond its small range into the heights and depths of the scale. The student has become a singer without intending to! The teacher is not surprised, as it has often happened before. The teacher did not make the voice. It must have been latent in the pupil. Without the proper means of bringing it out and building it up, it would have remained hidden forever. Freed from its physical prison and cultivated by a correct technique, it could not help but blossom.

The study of singing should not be the prerogative of the gifted, career-minded young student alone. Singing is a need for people of all ages. Singing lives as a half-conscious wish in many hearts, but age or lack of ability keeps people silent. The value of studying other art forms, regardless of one's age or capacity, is taken for granted. Thousands of people play instruments or paint or carve wood in their spare time, but singing lessons are usually seen as intended for those who are young and ambitious for a professional career. Singing, however, is actually necessary for everyone! It is more than an aesthetic activity, for the voice is a reflection of the human being, the hallmark of one's unique individuality.

Practice

The beginner who does hours of daily, unsupervised practice often undoes the work that has been accomplished with his teacher during the lesson. His concepts of word and tone are as yet unformed, and by repeating mistakes unknowingly at home, he will strengthen his wrong habits. Many great singers of the nineteenth and twentieth centuries knew this. Bonci (an Italian tenor of the Metropolitan Opera) said, "I regard practicing alone as a dangerous experiment." Caruso maintained, "Until they become thoroughly proficient in managing the voice, pupils should never devote more than fifteen minutes a day to practice."

Students are frequently urged to practice, as it is well known that instrumentalists practice many hours a day to improve their technique. This does not apply to the voice student. Ten-minute practice periods two or, at most, three times a day are enough in the beginning. Aimless practice leads nowhere. The teacher should explain the purpose of each exercise. Each ten-minute period should cover an important point and the exercise should be done with care and concentration, as much by the mind as by the voice. Musical *thinking* is important at this time. For a singer aiming at a career, limitless hours can be spent memorizing the texts of songs, mastering language difficulties, and reading the lives of the great song composers. But the actual use of the voice must never be casual or of great duration.

False Paths in Singing

○ The Pharynx Voice

When a word is pronounced in the upper throat, behind and above the mouth, the tone produced is more or less limited to the pharynx. Gracia Ricardo considered this method of voice training inadequate. The tone has little resonance and most of what it has is felt behind the soft palate. The singer's sensation is that the tone drifts upward through the cylinder of the throat and sings above the skull behind the crown. No strain is connected with it in any way, and its devotees admire its "naturalness and purity." But it is without carrying power or brilliance.

When the pharynx voice is used, the breath is borne along the wall of the throat without compression. It requires little support from the diaphragm. The breath stream, passing very far back in a straight column, is not allowed to fill the frontal cavities of the nose and head with tone. Mouth resonance is also forfeited. Not the slightest mixture of the lower registers is ever used. The lowest notes are frequently sung in the unmixed chest register unrelated to the rest of the voice.

A teacher practicing this method of voice training treats the voice like any other musical instrument, denying the singer's unique claim to be the bearer of the human word. When the voice is treated as if it were a flute, words are of little importance. The pharynx tone sometimes resembles a flute in quality, although it lacks the warmth of the flute's middle tones.

The pharynx tone uses the throat muscles throughout the scale in the way that is naturally employed in the production of only the very highest notes of every well-trained soprano. The pharynx singer has only this one limited position, this one way of singing, to see her through the entire vocal range. The voice is therefore inadequate in the low and middle registers.

When the highest notes are sung, the throat pillars are lengthened (and properly so) by drawing the veils of the soft palate up under the back of the nose. However, one should not be concerned with this physiological fact while singing. Singing should be free from consciousness of the physical activity of voice production. Physiology is concerned with muscles, ligaments, sinews, nerves and cartilage, which are all used in singing. General knowledge of their function is therefore appropriate, but we cannot feel any of these things when we sing or speak, and should make no effort to do so. The singer should be unaware of all that is going on in the larynx while singing. A too great concern with the anatomy of voice production may cause singing to become a purely physical act. The student may become too physically conscious to have the receptivity needed for the ringing, body-free etheric tone, and the voice will show it by becoming strained or hoarse, or by degenerating into mere sound. The position of the pillars and soft palate, properly used only in singing high tones, is retained throughout the vocal range of the pharynx singer. From a pedagogical standpoint, this tendency represents a serious misunderstanding of the developmental possibilities of the entire voice.

The pharynx singer remains a forever unfinished product. The potentialities of the voice are never realized. Only a small portion of its quality or quantity is ever heard. Although the pharynx tone is somewhat devitalized, it does not offend most people. To many it brings pleasure, and some consider it "spiritual." However, it can never be used as a satisfactory vehicle for song, which is a combination of words and music, because pure vowels cannot be produced in the pharynx. They must be formed by the organs of articulation and spoken on the lips, and pure vocal tone cannot be produced except through the medium of the vowel.

o The White Voice

When the pharynx singer feels inadequate to the demands made upon her voice, she usually does something about it. She must get more power and resonance at any cost, so she tries to focus her voice forward, not by the proper use of words, but by urging the tone into the high frontal cavities of the nose and head. No mouth resonance can be called into play because the position of the soft palate prevents the tone from entering the mouth and resounding against the hard palate. The tone is directed instead to the head resonators above. The voice is caught in the upper frontal cavities of the head, resulting in the "white voice."

Mathilde Marchesi, a famous voice teacher of the late nineteenth century, writes: "I recommend the practice of singing in Italian because this language carries the tone forward and prevents its being directed toward the soft palate. When the voice goes toward the soft palate the *voix blanche* or 'white voice' is the outcome. Pay no heed to those who advise you to practice with a smile, for this too gives the *voix blanche*."

Italian vowels do indeed bring the voice forward, as they are spoken on the front of the mouth and on the lips. Vowel purity predominates in Italian, and the purity of the vowel determines the freedom and beauty of the tone.

In *How to Sing*, Lilli Lehmann also has something to say about the white voice: "There are singers, male and female, who use too much head tone through their entire vocal range; such voices are called 'white.' In such cases it would be advisable to mingle judiciously with all the other vowels the vowel 'oo', which requires a lower position of the larynx. The voices would become warmer and would sound more expressive."

To free the pharynx singer from a limited use of the

resonators, there is certainly no better teaching device than the judicious mingling of the vowel "oo" with all the other vowels. Where this "oo" is concerned, however, we go even further. The "oo" does not merely require a lower position of the larynx, it provides one. If we sing or speak, or even merely think "oo," we will feel the larynx drop to a slightly lower position. If we do the same with "a," as in "late" or "mate", we will feel it rise higher than the normal position. This "a" sound produces the highest position of the larynx and "oo" the lowest. It is the control of the vowel, however, which moves the larynx up or down, and not the control of the larynx which influences the vowel. In using the vowel "oo," the singer relaxes the taut pillars and the raised soft palate to a normal position.

Reeducating the pharynx singer is an easy task. Results are always dramatic. In a few weeks the student begins to produce tones which use the resonators that were formerly cut off. The increased size of the voice is usually an astonishing revelation. One begins to have more use of the middle voice, which is the true medium of feeling, and one's expressive powers begin to assert themselves.

The students have not been asked to "begin all over." They have not been required to give up anything they have already attained. A new dimension has simply been added to their concept of singing. The ideal of bringing the quality of the upper voice into the lower voice is a sound one. It will be addressed in the chapter on "Blending the Registers." The pharynx singer does this very thing, but to an exaggerated degree. Actually, we must be taught to coordinate the registers through a sense of hearing. We will then be able to sing an equalized scale using a smooth blend of all three registers.

o The Glottal Action

When a tone is taken from below upward, the epiglottis, the movable lid at the top of the larynx, springs up and we feel the larynx. This is called the "glottal stroke." It sounds like the blow of a tiny hammer in the throat and occurs only on words beginning with a vowel. French singing teachers of the late nineteenth century used the term *coup de glotte* or "stroke of the glottis" as a synonym for the start of the tone. It has also been called a synonym for nearly all that is bad in voice production. While it is true that no musical sound can be produced without partially closing the glottis, that is, without bringing the edges of the vocal cords closer together, this action should not be prepared in advance. The partial closing of the glottis is the physical *result* of producing a tone and should not interest the singer from a physiological standpoint.

Although in some cases the vocal cords are strong and healthy enough to withstand the strain of this small explosion in the throat, it may in time produce nodules on the cords. To correct the glottal stroke, the singer should preface the initial vowel with the aspirant "h." In Lecture II of *Eurythmy as Visible Speech* ("The Character of Individual Sounds," June 25, 1924), Rudolf Steiner states that "h" is midway between consonants and vowels in relation to the breath. In fact, "h" is the breath itself. The aspirant "h" supplies enough breath so the vowel may be begun on the breath instead of with the throat muscles.

The glottal stroke, when employed *consciously*, may occasionally be used for effect in an operatic aria or song, but merely for dramatic enhancement. It should never be practiced regularly and its unconscious use should be pointed out and overcome.

Breathiness

Whereas in the glottal stroke the vocal cords are forced together, in the breathy tone they are kept too far apart. When we are silent, there is an almost round space between the two vocal cords. The glottis is then open. When we sigh, the breath pours freely past the cords, but they do not contract. The moment we speak or utter a sound they draw toward each other. The breathy tone resembles a sigh in that the air rushes out unused and the tone is diffused. This is much more difficult to correct than its opposite. The imagination of the consonant form helps keep the breath within bounds. Concentrating or focusing the word on the embouchure at the start of the tone is the best remedy. The important thing to keep in mind is that one should pronounce the word simultaneously with the tone, and not begin a tone and follow it with the pronunciation. The vowel should be imagined as very fine and small. To begin with, avoid exercises on the open vowel "ah." It is better to use "oo" until the fault is overcome. The control of the vowel "ah" can finally be achieved by beginning to vocalize on "oo" and working through "oh" and "aw." For example, the exercise *food, foot, foe, for, fob, far* sung on the easy middle notes of the scale which are usually used for daily speech, can bring about the balance of breath on the open vowel. It is on these middle tones that breathiness is most noticeable.

While breathiness cannot injure the vocal cords, it stands in the way of good singing. When the breath leaks out around the word, both word and tone lose the ability to retain a focal point, and the attainment of resonance and a legato line is impossible. As the breath is wasted, more must frequently be taken, and the singer is forced to break a song into fragments, thereby destroying the phrasing in order to take enough breaths. Breathiness is a problem of exhalation. For a time, it would be wise to sing sustained vocal exercises or songs softly, using only the middle voice, and setting a fairly long phrase as one's goal. Singing a long phrase by a careful expenditure of breath is often a matter of will power. If the breath is gone after a few measures, one must not take more and continue, but rather return to the beginning, watching more closely for its careful emission through the imaginary aperture on the lower lip (the embouchure). A "living" tone drinks in the small amount of breath it needs for support. In cultivating the breath this way, breathiness of tone, a most prevalent failing, can be corrected. The fault is one which is usually overcome by good training.

The Tongue

The tongue is the principal organ of diction and is controlled by the mind. It will not function properly when subjected to physical force. Only the tip can be controlled at will. In most people the tongue responds normally to the demands made upon it by correct pronunciation. If any abnormality in the action of the tongue exists, such as lisping, the student's attention should be drawn to it and the fault corrected, but as a rule mere mention of the tongue induces muscular tension in it. It must be allowed to lie flat on the floor of the mouth in singing all the vowels, with its tip resting lightly against the roots of the lower front teeth. Do not try to flatten it by force. If you relax the tongue together with the jaw, the tongue will find its proper place.

The Jaw

In muscular singing, the lower jaw sometimes moves at every change of pitch. Forcibly opening the jaws cramps the muscles of the throat and tongue, but jaw tension gives way when the breath stream is brought under control. A relaxed lower jaw is indispensable to good tone production because the freedom of the tongue and the larynx depends to a large extent on the freedom of the lower jaw. In its ideal condition the jaw, which is one of the resonators, should remain passive and relaxed, requiring no special attention.

The Lips

When the upper lip is pulled down and stiffened in an effort to control vowel formation, this is due to a misunderstanding on the part of the pupil. Formation and control of the vowels is connected not only with a delicate and sensitive response of the physical lips, but with the activity of the life forces in and around them. Exaggerated lip action is unnecessary and is, in fact, destructive, as it gives the vowels a static quality and imprisons them. The lip position does not form the vowel. The vowel forms the lip position.

Sometimes the lips are too loose. They hang flaccid and do not come around the word at all. On the other hand, the upper lip is often held in a straight, rigid line or a fixed smile. Then it cannot be of any use in the formative process. Another defect is the protrusion of the lips in the form of a trumpet. This distorts the words, and freedom of expression is impossible.

The lips should remain flexible, sensitive, and responsive to the demands of the vowels and consonants and to the play of feeling contained in the word. This is what the embouchure helps to achieve.

CHAPTER THREE

Blending the Vocal Registers

Webster's dictionary describes a register as:
A series of tones of like quality within the compass of a voice which are produced by a particular adjustment of the vocal cords. In singing up the scale the register changes at the point where the singer readjusts the vocal cords to reach the highest notes. All below this point is in the chest or thick register, all above it in the head or thin

register. The two registers generally overlap, some notes about the middle of the vocal range being producible by either.

Webster's recognizes two registers, but three exist. These can be compared to the three floors of a building: the basement, the main floor, and the steeple. They represent three disconnected ways of using the voice. Do registers exist by nature? Lilli Lehmann believed they were created through long years of speaking in the vocal range a person finds most comfortable, which then becomes a fixed habit. This habitual part of the voice grows strong in comparison with the others and forms the middle register. The series of tones below and above it are called the "chest" and "head" registers. This fixed habit of speech may indeed be an important contributing factor, but three registers can sometimes be heard in the singing of very young children.

A serious pitfall of the registers in the treble voice is the tendency to carry the low quality up into the middle range. If a singer starts the scale in the chest tones, and continues it upward as far as she can without allowing natural adjustments to take place in the larynx, she will notice a gradually increasing strain in the throat. If the fault is not corrected, permanent damage to some of the notes of the scale will surely follow. Describing his wife's (Jenny Lind's) voice, Goldschmidt said, "These three notes (F, G, A) were more seriously injured than any other region of the voice by the faulty method of production that had been forced upon Jenny Lind before her journey to Paris. It is well known to every experienced *maestro di canto* that more voices are injured by the attempt to sing these three important notes in the lower instead of the middle register than by any other error of production whatever, and there can be no doubt that it was this error that caused Jenny Lind so much trouble." Even after a period of intensive study with Manuel Garcia in Paris, which resulted in complete mastery of her instrument, Jenny Lind said that these three notes, abused in her youth, "never became quite right."

The singing voice is an expression of the threefold nature of the human being and within its compass we recognize thought, feeling, and will. The pure head tones are rather cold and convey little or no feeling. They are related to thought. The middle voice carries the message of the heart and is the vehicle of feeling. The chest voice manifests the will. Here deeds and dramatic power are expressed. The three parts of the voice must be blended into a homogeneous whole, produced evenly throughout the entire compass. The single, blended register is considered the sign of good singing. Where breaks occur, the voice is classed as poor and untrained.

The various groups of muscles used in the three registers and the difference in action of the vocal cords for head and chest tones are not the singer's concern. The singer's chief interest is the coordination of the registers through the development of a sense of hearing. Quality is the criterion here as elsewhere. The contralto, whose lower notes break into a register resembling the male voice, will, when her ear is trained to recognize it, know she is in vocal danger and will avoid the break between registers. By descending into her lowest tones with skill, she will realize their fullest possibilities, and the lowest notes, the "false chest tones" referred to above, will not rob the upper portions of the scale of their youth and health.

Although among singing teachers the blending of the registers has long been considered a trade secret, some have spoken of it openly. As early as 1223, John of Garland described the vocal registers and, in 1742, Tosi advocated working from the middle voice and extending the range in both directions. This is a good procedure for general voice cultivation where no breaks are noticeable. But when the change of registers is audible, the fault cannot be corrected by attention to the middle voice alone. The teacher should begin with the easiest high tones lying far above the break and carefully work down, as low as the voice will readily go. The "false chest voice" in women, which resembles masculine tones, should only be used occasionally and consciously for dramatic effect; it should never be produced or used in daily singing. The descent to the lowest notes should be a forward and downward path (like a waterfall or a miller's wheel). The voice should not be allowed to drop backward and down. There must be a feeling of space *below* the lowest tone as well as above it. Descending scales are the best exercises to bridge the breaks. A passage can be built— a stairway without platforms—leading downward from steeple to basement, along which the notes descend. They must never be forced up from below, but should always be *carried down from above*. The registers should not be trained separately with the hope that blending will automatically follow. It will not. Only by carrying the head voice into the middle voice and the middle voice into the chest voice will the necessary adjustment be made that enables the singer to produce an even scale using a blend of all three registers with ease and freedom. The cool tones of the upper voice are thus brought down into the middle register, to the soul sphere, which is the source of singing, and here they gain warmth and power of expression. Feeling is thereby manifested in the head register. By joining the two higher registers to the chest tones, the element of will is brought into the scale, which finally becomes a subtle blend of all three registers, having within it qualities of thought, feeling, and will.

Rudolf Steiner referred to the lowest tones as follows:

The actual musical experience reaches down only to the etheric body. Certainly the physical pushes upward into the lower tones. If, however, we were to go all the way down into the physical, the metabolism would be included in the musical experience, which would then cease to be a pure, musical experience.

Rudolf Steiner, *The Inner Nature of Music and the Experience of Tone* (Lecture V, Stuttgart, March 7, 1923)

Embellishments

It is difficult to understand why so many singers know little or nothing about the vocal embellishments. Nowadays, study of this aspect of singing seems to be limited to the education of the coloratura soprano.[2] *Every* voice needs embellishments. Quite apart from the demand for coloratura work in songs and arias of the present day, its pursuit should be encouraged because of the effect of all forms of scales and embellishments upon the control, beauty, and *elasticity* of the voice. Every voice is sometimes required to use embellishments; they should be so much a part of the singer's technical equipment that they are readily available for instant use whenever they appear in a score. Handel's *Messiah* which is sung so frequently, demands that the bass "shake all nations" on a slow coloratura, and he is expected to produce trills when describing "the refiner's fire." The contralto aria, "O Thou That Tellest Good Tidings to Zion," requires the flexibility usually asked only of a soprano voice, yet few basses and contraltos receive the schooling necessary for the performance of the embellishments.

o *The Grace Notes*

Various melodious vocal exercises for the grace notes exist

[2] A "coloratura" is a florid singer with particular flexibility. Today the term refers to the high-pitched female voice possessing particular ease in the upper range and a certain lightness throughout the voice, allowing for easy florid runs and embellishments. But coloratura or florid singing can also apply to the male voice within its own range, as well as to the contralto and dramatic soprano, who, especially in the earlier operatic works of Rossini, Donizetti, and Bellini, are required to sing many passages with great flexibility.

which are more interesting to the student than simple exercises. We find those by Marchesi and Vaccai the most useful. These booklets are limited to exercises for agility and embellishments. They treat the subject from a purely technical standpoint. The use of the voice in these exercises is the responsibility of the singing teacher.

○ The Portamento and Glissando

The *portamento* is often described as a gliding connection between two notes, but this more resembles the definition of a *slide*. The word "portamento" means "to carry." An example of a slide that is frequently regarded as a portamento occurs in the phrase "O... sometimes it causes me to tremble, tremble, tremble" in the Spiritual, "Were You There When They Crucified My Lord?"

In the true portamento the succeeding note is sung with the vowel of the preceding syllable. The new pitch must begin on the vowel of the preceding pitch.

An important point regarding the portamento is that the first note must arrive at the following note a trifle *before* it is time to sing the second note. The second pitch should be anticipated during the last instant of the preceding one. Sometimes the stress of the tone must diminish during the progress of the portamento, sometimes it must increase—but there must never be any alteration in the quality or color of the tone. Although the tone is carried through the intermediate notes, they should not be heard as separate pitches. If the portamento is taken from a purely tonal standpoint, sliding remains an ever-present danger, but when approached from the standpoint of vowel control, a true portamento can easily be won.

A *glissando* occurs when the singer sings from one pitch to another, allowing the voice to sound all the intermediate pitches. The glissando also has its place in vocal technique and can be very effective in songs and arias. Cyril Scott uses it in "The Blackbird's Song:"

Here all the pitches between G and E should be lightly touched and *sounded*. The result is a delicate, swift, chromatic glissando. As some songs call for a portamento and some for a glissando, it is necessary to know one from the other and to be able to produce either with equal skill.

○ *The Skip*

In addition to the portamento and glissando, the clean-cut interval called the "skip" should also be practiced. It is a necessary protection against the unconscious use of the portamento.

The "Messa di Voce"

The *messa di voce*, the note that swells and diminishes, is the epitome of technique and expression, combining the most extreme difficulties and subtleties of both. To surmount its exacting demands requires years of persistent study, as it is one of the major technical difficulties in the art of singing. Beginning with an almost inaudible tone, the singer must be able to swell the voice to a faultless climax and then reduce the amount of tone gradually while returning to the same softness of tone with which he began. The ability to constantly increase and decrease tone quantity while singing is indispensable to artistic finish—without it the greatest interpreter is helpless. Done well, the *messa di voce* is not usually noticed by the audience except when used for large, dramatic effects. When it is not done well, the voice is considered boring. It is the acid test for every singer and should be practiced with caution at first, and only in the voice's middle range. The sensation of a crescendo should not be one of pressure, but of expansion. The sensation of a diminuendo should be one not of contraction but of controlled relaxation.

The Vibrato, The Tremolo, The Trill

The vocal vibrato, as essential to good vocal tone as it is to good violin tone, should be present in every note the singer produces, but it should not be consciously heard by the untrained listener. It is a natural, smooth vibration which gives life and intensity to the voice. Where it is absent, the voice is wooden and expressionless.

The vibrato, a definite asset, should not be confused with the involuntary tremolo, which is a major vocal fault. The tremolo is the result of improper exhalation. Instead of streaming gently out through the lips, the breath is sent forcefully against the vocal cords, and even the strongest vocal apparatus cannot endure the uncontrolled physical pressure of the entire breath stream without suffering damage. The voice is bound to break under the strain, and the first sign of vocal degeneration is the tremolo. Instead of singing one pure tone after another, several pitches are set in motion at the same time on a single note. The tremolo has two forms: the trembling, unsteady, swiftly quivering tone that gives it its name, and the slow, quaking tone that deviates from the intended pitch. In both forms it is impossible for the singer to maintain a single steady tone. Correction of the fault is difficult and results are usually slow. The health of the vocal cords must be gradually restored by protecting them from the uncontrolled breath. The pupil is taught to emit breath through the cords in a small, steady stream, using only as much as is actually needed for the tone, and sympathetically and flexibly holding the rest in reserve.

To correct the tremolo, all vocal exercises should be practiced on the vowel "oo." This tends to steady a trembling tone and to prevent forcing in general. The pupil is also encouraged to anticipate a steady tone. He must inwardly hear the tone before singing it, and if his conception of the tone is steady, its production will improve.

The vocal trill is an acquired embellishment much demanded in music of the classical period. The singer acquires a trill in the same way as a portamento, an accacciatura, a mordant, or a turn —that is, by constant practice of these embellishments or grace notes, all of which add to the agility and elasticity of the voice. The trill is a rapid alternation of two separate pitches in the interval of a half tone, a whole tone, or a third. While the tremolo (the inability to maintain a steady tone) is a fault caused by poor exhalation and interfering tensions forcing the voice against the vocal cords, the trill is a conscious musical interval maintained on two quickly alternating pitches.

Every voice, even the basso profondo (the deepest male voice), needs to exercise for the trill. There is no better way of strengthening a voice for endurance than demanding the flexibility necessary for the performance of a perfect trill.

Resonance

The attainment of true resonance lies in singing or saying the word on the lips and allowing the resulting tone to fill the resonance chambers. Activating the resonators by driving words into them results in sound, but not in true tonal resonance. This hard, brittle noise is not only unpleasant, but destructive to the ear. The ear and eye function in opposite ways. The eye grasps an object and draws it into itself, but the ear bars the entrance of noise and physical sound. It tries to separate noise from etheric tone and to take in only etheric tone. It is an organ of reflection, and separates the pure etheric tone from that which is carried by the air. (See Rudolf Steiner, *The Inner Nature of Music and the Nature of Tone*.)

There is a widespread tendency to allow tone to degenerate into noise. Human beings are no longer as musical as they were in the past. One finds people today who actually enjoy the sound made by driving tone and word against the hard palate and into the bony cavities of the head. When this is done—and it is very prevalent—one does not hear tone at all, one hears bone! Many vocal methods are built upon this process. The distinction between forcing the voice into the head cavities, and allowing the tone, through its own activity, to fill these cavities and resound there, has been lost. The so-called mask placement of the voice is taught everywhere. Vocal exercises on consonant combinations like "ng," in the words such as singing, ringing, clinging, are used to draw the student's attention to the cavities behind the nose. The "ng" is forced into the "mask," or hollow bone cavities of the face, pulling the word and sometimes whole sentences up into the bony chambers of the head. This robs the resonators of their real purpose, which is to resound freely with tone. Often the "i" ("ee" like seed) in certain vocal exercises is also overstressed. It is a means of forcing the voice to resound in the head, as in the common exercise "mi, mi, mi, mi, mi," which one often hears backstage at the opera or before concerts—usually sung by nervous tenors. The forced use of the vowel sound "ee" exemplifies the complete misunderstanding of the vowel. Yet, when understood and used correctly, the vowel sound "ee" is truly the carrier of real resonance.

The natural resonance of "ee" should be in *every* vowel we sing. It is our starting point and runs through the entire song or vocal exercise from the first note to the last. "Ee" is the golden thread on which we string our pearls, the tones. It is the natural head resonance, the legato line, along which the melody flows. But when it is overdone, the voice becomes strident and cold. The gold turns to brass, and the voice takes on a raw edge; the singer frequently sings sharp, and although it may seem to him that he has gained power, he has actually lost tonal volume and quality.

What has happened is that, by using "ng" and "ee" to activate the bony cavities of his head, the singer has pulled his voice up by its own bootstraps, and now finds himself unable to control it beyond a certain point. The voice has also lost its individual character, and the singer tends to sound like everyone else who employs similar methods. One singing voice should never resemble another. Resonators differ as widely as faces or fingerprints, and each voice should be trained to bring out its unique and individual quality. Physical factors such as the resonating cavities of the head, the shape and position of the larynx and hard palate, and the size and form of the teeth all determine to a great extent the individual timbre of each voice and the natural beauty of the tone. A voice is, after all, only as beautiful as its resonators allow, but a mediocre voice can be enriched by the proper use of its physical attributes, and a beautiful voice can be reduced to stridency by their misuse.

When all the resonators are free of force or interference, pure tone results.

In many vocal methods, resonance is augmented by tension in the lower jaw. This results in a wooden tone, lacking vibrancy. In other methods, the cheeks play an important role, in which case we find the voice caught inside the mouth. Here enunciation occurs inside the mouth, instead of at the lips, and every vowel is distorted by the sound of "aw" surrounding it. A third method hurls or presses the voice from the back of the throat, using the throat muscles. This practice most endangers the health of the voice. Constriction of the throat muscles imprisons the voice, preventing the tonal resonance from radiating to all parts of the body. Conscious muscular action cannot improve resonance, which will occur only when all muscular interference is removed. True resonance and freedom of tone are not produced by conscious control of the muscles, but by a proper onset of the tone (a perfect attack) and by the ear, the mind, and the imagination of the singer.

The resonance chambers of a singer can be compared to those of a violin. The violinist produces tone, setting it free, the instant his fingers and the bow touch the string. The tone is not forced into the body of the violin but resounds there of its own accord. So the singer, speaking the word on the fine "violin string" of the lower lip (the embouchure) into its "acoustical shell," the imagined consonant form where it dwells, sets free a potentially unlimited tonal quality. This tone is balanced and sustained by the breath stream, which should resound by its own activity in all the cavities of the mouth, head, and chest. If allowed rather than forced to enter these chambers, the tone becomes less physical and more etheric. A singer's use of the physical body may nevertheless be compared with a violinist's use of the violin, for the etheric or life forces of the singer come into play here as they do in the arm and hand of the violinist. Active resonance, forcing the word and tone into the resonators, limits the sound to the singer's immediate surroundings. True resonance embraces not only the whole auditorium but links up with the universe and is limitless. It seems to exist in palpable form as far as it can be heard, and certainly continues to resound much farther. A body-free tone is not physical but spiritual, and knows no spatial limitation.

A singer's physical resonators are the pharynx, the lower jaw, the hard palate, the chest, the skull, the nasal cavities and frontal sinuses, and the spinal vertebrae near the shoulder blades. These make up the sounding board, which the singer must use with skill in speaking the word, allowing all the resonance chambers of the body to be free for tone. The singer must at all times use *all* available resonance. The tone must resound through head, back and chest, making the body a musical instrument and allowing not only the resonance cavities but the whole body to become a great resonance chamber: what Rudolf Steiner called "the lyre of the gods." This is a far cry from the cultivation of the "nasal resonance" advocated by many singing teachers today.

To come to a realization of the resonance in every tone is part of the subtle training in perception and hearing that every serious musician must undergo. For the singer, confidence in the vowel and in the embouchure (within a comfortable range of the voice) builds the ability to let the tone resound at the imaginary aperture on the lower lip where the vowel rests. This creates the foundation of true resonance. When this is done properly, the resonators are left free for the tone to resound. The tone is then increased, and should sound more resonant than the tone produced by driving the word against the physical resonators.

At a certain point in her career Gracia Ricardo, on tour in America, faced the problem of being accompanied by a greatly augmented symphony orchestra. Feeling that increased nasal resonance might be necessary against the tonal weight of sixty instruments, she asked a friend to take up the subject with

Rudolf Steiner. As Maria Renold reports, Steiner understood the situation perfectly and answered: "Nasal resonance is a very singular thing in that there is much that is wrong bound up with it. It is not a harmless matter. If a singer wants to develop nasal resonance it must be at the sacrifice of something else. To my mind, the tone loses its soul quality through this. The tone acquires too much vibrancy and becomes cold. Mme. Ricardo sings very musically and with a great deal of soul feeling and, in my opinion, does not need to alter her tone in any way. She has nothing to gain by it. On the contrary, I find it useless. The tone has, in itself, its natural portion of nasal resonance and that suffices." On another occasion Rudolf Steiner said of Gracia Ricardo: "She has the free tone."

Diction

Good diction is essential for perfect speech in singing. As we pointed out in earlier chapters, enunciation is a *formative* process in which the position and purity of the vowel determine the freedom and beauty of the tone. The noted Bel Canto master, Tosi, said in 1723: "Singers should not ignore the fact that it is the *words* that elevate them above the instrumentalists." Tosi permitted his students to work on the text of songs only after they had perfected all the vowels.

Today many teachers train the voice from a purely tonal standpoint, ignoring the importance of the words and treating the voice like any other musical instrument. They tell their pupils, "You may even have to sacrifice correct diction if by so doing you can best achieve beauty of tone." This is poor advice. In his book, *Interpretation in Song*, Greene writes:

All the singer's gifts, all his perfection of technique, all his observation of rules go for little or nothing if his singing is not *speech in song*. For this, he must have:

A. purity of diction;
B. a sense of prosody (the stress and intonation
   patterns of words) and meter;
C. similarity of quality in the sound of the spoken
   and the sung word.

Song is humanity's special gift, an attribute of the human being alone. Birdsong, for instance, is not related to human singing. The bird has no larynx. Its clear notes are not produced by drawing the vocal cords together, but result from movement, activity, flight. The skylark soars and, as it soars, it "sings"; and even the caged songbird moves about, flapping its wings, as it prepares to sing. But human singing is the result of inner and outer repose. A human being sings out of the quiet core of his being. Forms of movement, such as eurythmy, can help in the battle against tensions. Human song, however, is always preceded by a moment of complete inner tranquility and quiet.

The formation of pure vowels and consonants requires delicacy of touch. Bombastic or exaggerated pronunciation should be avoided. Clear pronunciation, however, is not enough. Gracia Ricardo attended a concert by a well-known soprano, famous for her clear diction. Afterward she said: "That is not what I mean by good diction. I would call it aggressive diction. In order to be understood she speaks the words at the sacrifice of everything else." For Mme. Ricardo, word, tone, and breath were the vocal trinity. She tried to awaken the student to an experience of the form and structure of the word, the metamorphosis of word into tone, and the living activity of the vibrating breath stream. The singer is an instrument through which the word and tone resound, but the words should not be thrust forward simply for the sake of clarity of meaning. This practice does violence to the melody. Understanding of the consonant form, and consciousness of the breath as the carrier of tone, overcome the tendency to "speak in the throat," that is, to use the throat muscles for articulation.

Consonants, which have often been called "interrupters" of the tone, should be so quickly spoken that the legato line remains unbroken. Yet they must retain their identity as consonants and not tend to become vowels. Try to sing the almost impossible phrase from *Der Freischutz*, "Täuscht das Licht des Monds mich nicht," on a single tone, giving each consonant its full value, yet retaining legato throughout. It can be done! First determine the sustained sound in each word. In this way you anticipate the vowel sound in every word. You are not singing consonants, but vowels. Consonants are spoken. Vowels are sung. That is, they become tone. The first consonant "T" provides the imagination of the form for the whole sentence. The other consonants should be neither stressed nor ignored. The object should be to get them out of the way so the vowel will have a chance to sing.

Reading aloud, exaggerating all the consonants until distinctness becomes habitual, is an excellent exercise. After a time, the exaggeration must be dropped, but the clarity of the consonants will remain.

Words should not be studied merely for mechanical precision. The student should also attain a thorough understanding of their meaning and mood. Read the text of your songs as you would a poem. Pronounce the words simply and without affectation on the lowest comfortable pitch, avoiding any artificial style. Absorb the content of the poem. Speak "on the breath," without interference from any of the muscles of the throat. If the words are overpronounced and the vowels fail to stand up against the consonants which follow the vowels, a caricature of the truly spoken word results. Join the words together in a flowing phrase. The result is vocal continuity in which one vowel flows into the other. When a legato is established, intone the word on one note as you read: now you are *chanting*. This will solve many problems of diction. When you are able to apply this technique to the rising and falling pitches of a song, you will find that clarity and evenness, a "similarity of quality in the sound of the spoken and the sung word," have been attained. The difference between such reading and true singing is so slight as to be practically nonexistent!

A singer's diction may be influenced by daily speaking habits. These should be modified to suit the requirements of singing. Although artificiality must be avoided in pronouncing the sung word, the casual pronunciation of daily speech is unsuitable for singing. In singing, the word must regain its dignity.

High Notes

By high notes, we mean the tones that belong in the uppermost register, the register farthest above the natural speaking range, of every voice. In the female voice this is called the "head voice."

Some teachers maintain that less breath pressure is needed to sing the high treble tones just as less bow pressure is required to produce the high notes of a violin. Others say that since high notes are sung with greater intensity, breath pressure should be increased as the tones ascend.

But it is not a question of breath pressure at all. Using only as much breath as is needed, the singer should allow the high tones to sing themselves using only as much breath as is needed. One must not prepare for the high notes beforehand but should be *surprised* to hear them. The less one does, the more one has! Power comes through expectant calm. High notes result from a mood of quiet expectation. They are the flower of controlled relaxation. By helping the high tones the pupil will bring a physical urge or effort into their production, and muscular aid is not a help but a hindrance. In the treble voice, the perfect upper note sings itself! We do not sing it. It sings us!

On the highest notes of all voices, the vowel should be spoken into the consonant form, finished, and allowed to go off into tone much more quickly than in the middle and low notes. In "tossing off" the top notes, the student should feel that the *place* of speech is a trifle farther out or farther away in space from the physical lips than it is for the rest of the scale. The enunciation and finishing of the vowel and its transformation into tone are instantaneous!

If the vowel tends to spread or to become too open in ascending the scale, think of "oo." Thinking "oo" into the high notes, keeps the tone from fanning out. "Oo" forms a natural groove, adds color and richness, and reduces the possibility of physical strain. Singing into the "dome of oo" is called "covering" or "sombering" the voice. Although it is used in all voices, it is most essential for the male voice. If the male sings "open" to the top of this range, the upper tones resemble a shout. The "dome of oo" prevents this. The male voice also has the tendency to flicker or "break" just where the upper register-change occurs. The male singer has the choice of singing the top notes in the male head register or of breaking into the treble register, called the falsetto. Though formerly in good repute, the falsetto is frowned upon today and is never used in its pure, unmixed form except for special effects. Some modern music demands its use, such as the role of the Captain in Alban Berg's opera *Wozzek*. The unmixed falsetto of the bass is the countertenor. With the "dome of oo" as his goal, the singer can learn to enter the highest male register without flickering or breaking. His top notes will be firm, round and steady. The "dome of oo" is also a valuable aid in avoiding vowel distortions in the high notes of all voices. In many songs, the highest note is sung on a closed vowel.

It is not easy for students to realize that to sing high notes one must not reach up for them. The teacher should explain that in singing up an octave one is mentally going down. In the following exercise, for instance:

Oh———————

At the higher E, one should think of dropping the word "oh" to the floor! The gesture of the high notes should be a *downward* gesture. All the preceding tones, of course, must be properly formed and "in place". Each preceding tone is the springboard for the higher tone which follows. Keeping the downward gesture in mind, the following exercises for high notes can be helpful. They may be transposed to every key and should be sung on all vowels.

O *Exercises for High Notes*

Exercise 1

Exercise 2

Exercise 3

1. Bu --- bu — bu — bu — bu
2. Bo ---- bo — bo — bo — bo

1. Bu — bu — bu — bu — bu
2. Bo — bo — bo — bo — bo

1. Bu — bu — bu — bu — bu
2. Bo — bo — bo — bo — bo

1. Bu — bu — bu — bu — bu
2. Bo — bo — bo — bo — bo

On all vowels as high as the voice will comfortably go.

Exercise 4

1. Bu — bu — bu — bu — bu — bu — bu
2. Bo — bo — bo — bo — bo — bo — bo

On all vowels as high the voice will comfortably go.

Exercise 5
(only after a certain ease and proficiency has been attained)

On all vowels as high as the voice will
comfortably go.

Then, on "ah" and "oh" (without the consonant).

Exercise 6
(for the advanced student)

In this particular exercise, the first section *passes* the highest note without holding it; the second *touches* and *repeats* it lightly; the third *holds* it briefly and the fourth *sustains* it.

The Ear

Can a singer depend upon the ear as a guide to tone production? Eventually, yes! The ear and voice are inseparable, and learning to sing consists largely in cultivating tonal discrimination by means of the ear. But only a carefully trained ear is dependable! Nearly every beginner has preconceived opinions concerning his voice and how it should be used to achieve what he considers the best results. People who sing through the nose sometimes believe their tones are "pure velvet." Others, who clutch the tone with their throat muscles, secretly consider their voices to be brilliant. They simply cannot hear. If a tone is loud and resonant around his own ears, the singer thinks it must also be so in the rear of the auditorium; but the tone that can nearly deafen a person standing next to the singer may be so deficient in overtones as to be practically inaudible beyond the third row. We must strive for vocal self-knowledge! The pupil must learn to listen objectively. We must learn to hear our own voice as though it were the voice of another and judge quite impersonally. Vocal tone is not merely pitch or sound. It is a spiritual reality. Until our ear can recognize, and our mind can conceive, a tone free from physical interference, we cannot be sure that we are singing a free tone.

At first, as pupils, we must rely on the teacher's ear and we frequently fail to notice the difference between the teacher's example and what we are producing. An "oh" continues to be "ow" and we cannot hear the difference. A student's deafness to her own faulty articulation is not easily overcome. The perfect vowel is at first far removed from her field of consciousness. To tune the ear to the subtle difference requires infinite patience. It is a red-letter day for the singer when she hears the fault and corrects it. For when she produces a pure vowel within its consonant form, she will hear her real voice for the first time. This is always a thrilling surprise. If her ear experiences this just once she will never again be satisfied with anything less but will pursue perfection as long as she lives. The ear which has become sensitive is the singer's greatest ally. Lilli Lehmann writes, "Learn to hear yourself. Perfect tone involves a complex coordination which can only be controlled by the ear. Singing is devoid of physical sensation and can only be controlled indirectly by *listening*."

Rudolf Steiner refers to the ear as the human being's most spiritual organ. In the embryo, the ear lies far from the pull of earth. The ear is all that remains of the capacity to perceive the harmony of the spheres. The human being experiences in earthly tones a feeble reflection of that creative world out of which he has been molded. The ear points to the past. The larynx points to the future and will become a most significant organ in human evolution.

When listening is changed from a quantitative to a qualitative experience, an inner tone sense will awaken. No muscular training of the vocal organs can produce this inner hearing. By cultivating inner hearing, or qualitative listening, the singer enriches his art and opens his own door to the spirit. He presses through the sensible and becomes an instrument able to perceive beyond it. The inner tone sense awakens, giving access to a spiritual world order which is the basis of all artistic creation.

The art of singing connects past and future. The ear and the larynx are used simultaneously. This inner hearing transcends the function of the ear. It becomes the sensitive, supersensible "sense of tone."

CHAPTER FOUR

(for the Professional or Aspiring Singer)

Choosing a Program

Creating a program is an art in itself. There is an abundance of vocal literature; in fact, the masterpieces of song are inexhaustible—the field is limitless. But choosing songs for a concert is a great responsibility. An audience comes not only to hear a singer's voice or to be entertained, but to temporarily forget their personal burdens and to be lifted up to a higher realm of experience.

We should choose a program of songs based on poems that are especially meaningful to us. A personal connection is important. Some great songs are unusable by certain singers because the words do not suit their temperament. For instance, not everyone can sing Ravel's "Chanson de Madagasque." If a singer feels unequal to the demands of a poem, or has an antipathy toward it, the song should not be sung. The time may come when we will feel able to sing it. The worth of a song, however, is not dependent on its content. A good poem with poor music does not make a good song. When a beautiful poem is set to fine music, a work of art is created.

As a rule, there is no place on the recital program for an operatic aria. When an opera singer gives a concert, she is expected to sing arias and is happy to fall back on what she does best. Concerts are not really her field and, as a rule, there are few opera singers who also excel as concert singers. The opera singer is accustomed to costume, light, freedom of movement, colorful pageantry, acting, and the accompaniment of an orchestra to aid in the portrayal of a role. A concert singer is alone with an accompanist and a piano and portrays many roles in the course of an evening.

Good concert programs are the result of research and study. In addition to the classical repertoire, other songs should be offered. It takes time to discover the unusual. It is sometimes said that audiences prefer to hear what they know, but it becomes increasingly obvious that audiences long for new musical experiences. The hackneyed song can be boring even when sung by a master singer. Try to offer something out of the ordinary.

Listeners should also be treated to a frequent change of mood. There are several moods to choose from—for instance, the contemplative, the humorous, the reminiscent, and the narrative. Choose a variety of moods for each song group.

Change of key is important. It is tiresome to hear several songs in the same key. For the same reason, do not follow a song in a minor key with another minor, unless there is an artistic reason for it.

In the nineteenth century most songs were composed in 4/4 or 3/4 time. When programming songs of the romantic period, try to vary the time signatures so a piece in 4/4 is followed by one in 3/4 and not by another in the same rhythm. Nowadays, as in earlier music, many time changes occur in the same song and one is freed from the repetition of the 4/4 or 3/4 beat.

Stage Fright

One of the worst causes of poor performance is stage fright, that dreadful nervous malady well known to almost every singer. The public does not want to hear a frightened artist. Stage fright is an intense form of self-consciousness, a manifestation of egoism. A *little* nervousness is a good thing. The singer who is incapable of some nervousness is lacking in the sensitivity necessary to an artist, but in its worst form, stage fright paralyzes the vocal cords, disrupts the breathing, and cramps the imagination. If the singer puts his art before the selfish fear that possesses him, stage fright can be overcome.

Song Interpretation

By the time the singer reaches the sphere of interpretation, technical skill must be taken for granted. All analysis must be avoided during performance. Until one has learned to handle one's voice without consciously thinking about it, interpretation, in its fullest sense, is impossible. Interpretation is the *height* of the singer's art. Through it, one must convey human experience and imagination. What the singer has not directly experienced, she must be able to imagine, and interpretation's chief ingredient is imagination. The singer must find the means of communicating her experience and imagination, transformed into art, to her listeners. To help her, she has the world's most beautiful poetry, written about every human emotion, lifted up and objectified by music. To depict human experience in song is the singer's highest objective. In fact, it is sometimes said that singing is motivated by the singer's desire to communicate to the world the intimate, individual feelings inherent in the song which she is convinced she can present by her special understanding.

It is certainly true that in interpretation the personality and individuality of a singer begin to emerge. The singer comes of age. Interpretation is a never-ending process of growth. Years of experience are needed to attain it, and one's achievements are never final. Experience is the great teacher, and that is the one thing even the most gifted young singer lacks. Through the years, the artist gradually learns to shake off restraints and fettering inhibitions, and to stand before an audience as an unself-conscious vehicle for bringing the song and its message to life. The singer may then become the clear crystal, through which a greater light may shine.

The Mood

In interpretation the artist must forget himself and assume for the moment the character he is portraying. The singer is sometimes accused (and often justly) of being too subjective, of expressing himself! Surely the art of singing should express something higher than the limited personal qualities of the singer. Everyone has had the experience of hearing a singer, perhaps with a very beautiful voice, whose interpretation was so subjective, and therefore so sentimental, as to be almost unendurable. How can one overcome this? By establishing the mood of the song and inwardly identifying oneself with the person the song is about. The singer may be absorbed by various personal problems or pleasures as he steps out to sing. Perhaps he has just had some accident, or a session with the dentist, or has won the lottery, or has a cold and hopes it won't show, or he may have just signed a good contract. All this must be laid aside during the concert. He must lift himself out of the events of daily life into the realm of imagination and the universal human.

By the end of the concert, consisting usually of about twenty songs, the singer will have portrayed almost all the human emotions, but to no avail if he has not helped his audience to experience them. If the audience has not been inwardly enriched by a deep human experience, or charmed and uplifted, the singer has failed. Applause alone is not the barometer. A sympathetic current should flow between singer and listener. How often do singers who are great vocal technicians receive enthusiastic applause merely for their technical achievements. Some are able to sustain unusually long phrases without breathing, others are admired for their outstanding vocal flexibility and agility, or for their E above high C. But when one carefully examines the work of some of these singers, there seems to be a striking difference between their effects and those of the singer "who has something to say." A singer should sing *with* effect, not *for* effect. There is something chilling about mere technical perfection; technique is only the vehicle for art. The singer who does not take the last step in his artistic development has missed the highest ideal of his professional life. It is even possible to attain fame without artistic growth. Success in an artistic sense is not an outward manifestation; it is an inward realization. The singer *knows* when the audience has experienced the full meaning of a song with him. As Lawrence Tibbett, the great American baritone, once said, "An artist is not merely an emitter of high C's; he is a medium through which musical communication must flow." The singer's aim is to be the means through which the universal human can be experienced by each one present through the medium of song.

Understanding the Song

Success in interpretation depends upon the singer's capacity to absorb a song's deepest meaning. A singer who cannot grasp this meaning will never move her audience. Once she has it, magic will come alive between them. Understanding is the key to interpretation; a singer cannot interpret something she does not understand. Understanding depends upon the artist's spiritual development. Until one acquires the sensitivity that makes one human being aware of the soul needs of another, one will not be able to communicate the subtleties of the human soul to one's listeners. Human values should be the singer's chief concern. The ability to lay aside personal tensions, to immerse oneself in the mood of the song, and to objectify the subjective constitutes the highest form of interpretation. The artist's task is summed up by Suzanne Langer in her book *Problems of Art*. She writes: "In art we don't want self-expression! The artist objectifies the subjective realm. What he expresses is therefore not his own feelings, but *what he knows about human feeling*."

Word Painting

Gracia Ricardo called interpretation by means of the word, divorced from its context, "word painting." For example, in Dunhill's setting of the poem " The Cloths of Heaven" by W.B. Yeats, the words used to describe the cloths should be sung according to their meaning, apart from what they are describing. "The *blue* and the *dim* and the *dark* cloths of *night* and *light* and the *half-light*." The blue is *blue* whether it describes the sea, the beloved's eyes, a cornflower, or the cloths of heaven. The singer should interpret *blue* regardless of its context. There is a difference between *dim* and *dark* which can be brought out, just as there is between *night* and *light* and the *half-light*. Such painting of words in color overcomes subjectivity and lends variety even to the single phrase. If one interprets words freed from their context, they are taken away from the realm of thinking and brought into the realm of true feeling, which is the source of real interpretation.

A warning is necessary here. Word painting is not for beginners. Fascinated by the quality and content of separate words, the inexperienced singer may be lost in a morass of unimportant detail and be unable to see the woods for the trees! She may forget that the song is, after all, a musical work. Over-elaboration can monopolize a student's interest to the detriment of the atmosphere of the song as a whole. The desire to find effects to put into a song should be changed to a healthy interest in what can be drawn out of it. A song is more than a poem, it is also a piece of music, and the communication of musical ideas is a large part of song interpretation. Interpretation of song is the faithful rendering of the intentions of both the poet and the composer.

The musical phrase should, however, always be governed by the poem. This is not always done. It is inconceivable that the notes of a song be set down and then a suitable poem chosen for the musical composition. It is the other way around. The composer selects a poem, then sets it to music. In the songs of the great composers, the highlight of the music corresponds to the master phrase of the poem. In the works of lesser composers, the singer is sometimes frustrated by a lack of union between the two. In that case, the master phrase of the poem should be honored, and the musical high point must fall by the wayside.

Singing through the Silence

It has been said that the singer must be singing mentally before she utters the first word of a song. This is doubly true of rests and interludes when she is outwardly silent. She must continue to sing inwardly and to carry her listeners in the mood of the song through all the moments of vocal silence. She should maintain unbroken continuity from the introduction of the song to its termination.

From the moment she lays aside the workaday world and lifts herself into the realm of imagination, the singer must begin, mentally, to sing. At this first moment the singer stands and waits. The audience may wonder what the artist is waiting for. Is it for the latecomer to be seated, for quiet attention to prevail? Partly, but most of all one is waiting for the right inner moment to start. One stands in quiet expectation, waiting to "be sung." Once the mood of the song is experienced, the music surrounds us and rises from within. Mentally, a singer begins to sing the moment the accompanist plays the first note, and sings silently through the piano introduction, the rests, and the postlude, to the very last moment of the last note—and even a trifle longer.

Stage Presence

The human being is the only living creature who stands upright by means of his vertical spine. His posture on stage should reflect human dignity and equilibrium. Traditionally, the singer's weight is thrown upon the ball of the right foot while the left foot, with raised heel, is slightly behind. For most people this position brings the body into comfortable equilibrium, but some feel a better balance when both feet, side by side, are flat on the floor. Each singer must find his own stance.

The shoulders should be relaxed. The head should be held at a level that would enable the singer to look into the eyes of someone his own height standing directly in front of him. The chin should be neither lifted nor lowered. Raising the head to look up while singing affects the neck muscles, closes the throat, and can mar the tone quality.

The hands should hang at the sides or be held together simply, and anything resembling restlessness should be avoided. The more quietly a singer stands, the more impressive his bearing. One must be self-possessed and sure of oneself and this should show, though modestly, in one's general appearance.

A calm facial expression is an asset to the public singer. The singer's consciousness must have a content before he starts to sing. If it does not, there is the danger he may slip into mediumistic singing. The point is to bring into imaginative conscio usness what lives in the depths of the soul. The singer's task is to lift those universal human experiences in which every human being can share into an objective realm.

Whether a song expresses a mother's love, the experience of death, or the loss of a beloved, singing objectifies experience so that everyone may feel it—not so much on a personal level but, by means of art, and still intensely, on a more objective level. It is this kind of artistic experience which unites human hearts and lifts them out of the everyday world to a higher realm of human experience. In this realm one can have an inkling of the divine in the human being.

AFTERWORD

Esoteric Aspects of Music and Singing

MUSIC—if it is true music—has its origin in the spiritual world, not in the physical world that surrounds us. Other forms of art, such as architecture, sculpture, and even painting, have their archetypes in the world we see around us. But the melodies, harmonies, and rhythms that we experience in the music of our great composers are "faithful copies of the world of Devachan." We all experience them in deep sleep and in our journey from death to rebirth. Those whom we call composers have the ability to re-create these melodies, harmonies, and rhythms, and to help us experience them in earthly life. When we hear great music, something in us knows that we have our origin in other worlds. We are reminded of what we experienced there. In this sense, listening to music, whether we are aware of it or not, is a religious experience. (Religious in the sense of *religo*, *religare*—that which binds us once more with the world from which we came, the world of spirit: relinks us with God.)

Music consists of melody, harmony, and rhythm. These components are forces that exist within the human being as well. Melody is related to the head, to the activity of thinking, although it can never become thinking as such. Just as we speak of a "sequence of thought," we can also speak of a "sequence of melody." We follow a melody sequence with the same forces that we use for thinking. But in music this activity must never become thinking, otherwise it would cease to be music. Thus we can say that melody is a kind of held-back thinking. It does not quite become thinking, but is held back, arrested. This is the experience of melody in the human being.

90

Rhythm is related to the limbs and to the activity of the will. We know that when we experience music with a predominantly rhythmical quality, we want to tap our foot, or even our finger or hand. But we will tend for the most part to hold this back. Were we to succumb fully to the music in its rhythmical force, rhythm would become external movement. Holding back the outer movement allows us to experience the movement within, as music. Rhythm is therefore a kind of held-back willing, which "gets caught up in the limbs" (Steiner). Though we feel it primarily in the limbs, it is experienced, of course, throughout our being. Rhythm truly is arrested willing. If it became will, and thrust itself into action, became action, it too would cease to be music.

So melody is held-back thinking and rhythm is held-back willing—held back, but *alive* as force within the human being. And harmony? Harmony is experienced in the middle region of the human being. Harmony enters the heart directly and is experienced as feeling. Related to feeling, and uniting with melody and rhythm, harmony brings a balance into the human soul.

Music enters human experience directly through the heart as harmony. It rises into the head and is there experienced as melody. As Rudolf Steiner points out, the head's ability to experience melody makes it accessible to feeling. Otherwise the head would only be accessible to concepts.

Let us look at this seemingly radical statement. Music helps keep us human. Take a brilliant person whose brain is capable of penetrating the most complex engineering problems. Were it not for the humanizing element of music, which is experienced in the head as melody, the head would cease to be accessible to anything but cold facts, concepts. Music, experienced by the head, makes it receptive to human feeling.

Music descends into the limbs and is experienced there as rhythm. Melody, harmony, and rhythm (head, heart, and limbs) form the whole human being, the *spiritual* being. When we experience music in a true sense, we bring a harmonizing, unifying, balance to expression in the soul. Music, if it is true music, makes us whole.

If we can accept the notion of purpose in the great impulses of humanity, then it will not be hard to accept the statement that Rudolf Steiner makes regarding the task of music. The task of music is to make us human, in the higher sense of our humanity. Rudolf Steiner said, "If it were not for music, frightful forces would rise up in man." Shakespeare shows a sense for this when Lorenzo, in *The Merchant of Venice*, says:

> The man who hath not music in himself,
> Nor is not moved with concord of sweet sounds,
> Is fit for treasons stratagems and spoils;
> . . . .
> Let no such man be trusted.

"Treasons, stratagems, and spoils,"—or, as Rudolf Steiner described them, treason, murder, and deceit—exist in each of us. (A now obsolete meaning of the word "stratagem" is "bloody deed of violence." "Murder" is therefore an appropriate substitution.) Truly "frightful forces"—treason, murder, and deceit—or to use the more concrete, less "watered down," terms that Steiner attributes to the teachers of the ancient mystery centers—serpent, wolf, and fox—live in each of us. But we have the power of music to ward off these forces and to subdue their effects upon us. Serpent, wolf, and fox live in every human being; and music is there to counteract these forces in us.

Spiritual science tells us that melody, harmony, and rhythm are the expression of the three aspects of our being (head, heart, and limbs) and that they correspond to particular instruments of the orchestra. *Melody* is represented primarily by the winds. The primary function of wind instruments such as the flute and clarinet in a full orchestra is to carry a melodic theme. (A single wind instrument cannot produce harmony by itself.) *Harmony* is represented by the strings. The harmony in a full orchestra is produced primarily by the string section. *Rhythm* is represented by the percussion instruments. Thus the orchestra consists of winds, strings, and percussion—that is, melody, harmony, and rhythm—or head, heart, and limbs—and is an expression, an image, of the whole human being.

But what of singing? What is singing, and why is it important? The experience of music connects us with spiritual worlds. We are reminded of our source, our place of origin. Furthermore, when we play an instrument or hear it played, soul vibrations are set in motion that have an enlivening, uplifting effect on the soul and, thereby, a health-giving effect on the body. The instruments most capable of affecting us in this way are those that respond most directly to human influence, namely the strings (violin, viola, cello) and the wind instruments or instruments of the breath (flute, recorder, oboe, horn, etc.). When we sing, however, we ourselves are the instrument. It is important that we sing, but—if we wish to bring about the most beneficial effects on our body, soul, and spirit—<u>how</u> we sing is even more important.

Rudolf Steiner's suggestion was that we must acquire a greater awareness of what the air is doing in its movement in and around us when we sing. Diverting our attention from the physical organs to the movement of the air leads us to an understanding of the etheric element in singing. This etheric element is what singing must aim at more and more. Yet it must be clearly understood that the etheric element and the air are not the same. The air is material, the etheric spiritual. But through the movement of the air in singing one can begin to have an inkling of the etheric.

Singing freely is not a question so much of loud or soft singing as of freedom in the tone, a freedom from physical constriction that allows the tones actually to come to play on the instrument of the body, freely and flexibly. Few people can achieve this freedom naturally. Adults can learn it through a conscious study. Children, however, can learn it only by imitating those who do it well. Today it is imperative that we learn to find—consciously—this freedom in singing. The tensions of our age constantly threaten this freedom, and we will find ever more frequently that physical and emotional rigidities tighten our throats and other parts of our singing organism, making it increasingly difficult to sing at all.

And it is important that we sing. It is especially important for our children to sing. Singing frees the soul, makes it flexible, and helps it soar and expand. Singing lets the sun in—gives warmth to our lives and wings to our spirit. Those who sing know this. To sing at all requires a certain degree of freedom. Learning to sing in the way described here means finding ever higher degrees of freedom in ourselves. When we sing with this freedom, we find ourselves anew. When we sing with others, we find one another. Singing music that lifts our souls in freedom, we open ourselves to worlds that fructify the spirit in us. We make our souls flexible and receptive to spiritual worlds—open to what the spiritual worlds can tell us.

Correct singing leads us to an awareness of inner coordination, inner balances, the inner and outer worlds of tone, the heights and depths of our own being. Singing is such an intimate matter, bound up with one of the most intimate aspects of ourselves—the voice—that we can hardly enter the realm of song without touching upon the deepest realities. Singing is a holy path. A student would do well to travel the path only with those who realize that the task of learning to sing goes far beyond a mechanistic comprehension of the voice.

Singing enriches, ennobles, and strengthens the soul, and contributes greatly to the search for our own sense of self in its highest form. Yet, for all this, singing is also the simplest form of joy that we can experience.

APPENDICES

I

GRACIA RICARDO, AMERICAN SOPRANO

March 14, 1870— September 28, 1955

Gracia Ricardo's soul was universal and prompted her to bring her message of singing not only to her native country, but to foreign lands as well. She was born Grace Richards in Montclair, New Jersey, on March 14, 1870. Her father, J. Handley Richards, was publisher of the *New York Evening Post* and also president of Cooper Union, a prestigious tuition-free undergraduate college in New York City. He arranged for Abraham Lincoln to speak there—an act which led to Lincoln's nomination for the presidency. Her mother, Frances Baker, was a direct descendant of Samuel Adams, who was the older, more retiring cousin of John Quincy Adams, president of the United States.

Grace Richards graduated from Metropolitan New York College of Music in 1892. Following her graduation, she went to Hawaii to be with her favorite brother, Theodore, then president and choral conductor of Kamehameha School (the chartered school for Hawaiians). In 1895, she replaced him as choral conductor, thereby releasing him for more academic and athletic work at the school. While in Honolulu she married Ralph Woodward, a teacher at the school. One of her first opportunities as a truly professional musician also came to her in Honolulu when her friend, Governor Dole, the first governor of the Islands, asked her to sing the national anthem at the official ceremonies for the Islands' annexation to the United States in 1898.

Throughout her college days in New York, Grace Richards' ardent wish had been to study voice abroad. This wish was granted. She left Hawaii for Europe where she studied first with Sbriglia in Paris and later with Lilli Lehmann in Berlin, and became the friend of the composer Johannes Brahms, who coached her in his songs. By 1905, she was well known as a concert singer in Europe, touring with the renowned violinist Jan Kubelik and many other eminent musicians, including Ernestine Schumann-Heink, a famous mezzo soprano of the Metropolitan Opera. Besides Britain and the European continent, she also toured Russia and the Balkan countries with outstanding success. It was this concertizing that prompted her to Italianize her name to Gracia Ricardo, a practice customary for singers at that time.

The following are samples of some of her concert reviews during the years 1905-1908:

Gracia Ricardo, the young American, trained in Paris and Italy, who accompanied Kubelik on his recent autumn tour in England, made an unusually successful appearance in Dresden at the Musenhaus. Her voice, a soprano of much sweetness and flexibility, has been very carefully trained and she sings with great taste. The result is charming in its delicate simplicity and refinement.

Dresden Continental Times

Madame Ricardo had a most remarkable success in the Salle des Agricultures last night. The large and elegant audience accorded the singer an ovation, and listened with great pleasure to her beautiful voice and unusual vocal art.

Le Figaro (Paris)

Madame Ricardo's singing, which is not unknown to New York, gave her listeners pleasure, in its pleasing style and unaffected manner of singing. She sings with intelligence and with an appreciation of the varied significance of her music. Her diction is good, and her phrasing merits praise.

The *New York Times*

It is also interesting to note that while developing his phonograph, Thomas Edison (1847-1931) asked his friend Gracia Ricardo to record her singing for him. After listening to the result, he remarked disappointedly, "You can't can roses."

The following anecdote, reported by Maria Neuscheller Renold, is characteristic of Gracia Ricardo's personality:

Gracia Ricardo had been introduced at the Court of St. James in London as Mrs. Woodward. She was frequently invited to affairs of all kinds in aristocratic homes. On one such occasion, however, she had been invited to sing. When she arrived at the house and the butler asked her name, she replied, "Gracia Ricardo." As one of the artists, she was promptly ushered into the servants' quarters, where she found the other members of the ensemble. That is where artists were sent! Time passed, when suddenly a very agitated hostess appeared. "But Mrs. Woodward, we have been looking for you everywhere. Won't you please come into the parlor and join the guests?" "Thank you," Gracia Ricardo replied, "but today I am Gracia Ricardo. I will gladly come if my fellow artists are also invited." They were!

Hildo Deighton, in her book *Early Days of Anthropsophy*, wrote of Gracia Ricardo:

When I first knew her, she was a majestic and commanding figure, a cosmopolitan personality, in the spiritual sense of the word. She had a warrior's bravery, a strong will, and a warm heart. When she took a firm stand, she was not easily swayed. She spoke her mind freely and expected others to do the same. If her anger was aroused, it rarely lasted overnight, as she had a forgiving nature and suffered over not always meeting this in others. She tried to begin each day as a clean slate, harboring no ill will. Feeling a deep need for affection herself, she gave of it unstintingly to her friends.... She had been the only girl in a family of three boys and so had been allowed almost anything she wanted, and what she wanted most was to sing. Early pictures of her show a tall, handsome girl, carefree and full of fun.

During 1908, while in Berlin, she was introduced to Rudolf Steiner and became a serious student of his spiritual science. Prior to a recital, Steiner would frequently lead her by the arm up to the podium of the Bechstein Saal in Berlin. Despite her musical activity and tours her devotion to anthroposophy and to Rudolf Steiner never took second place. She became a very dear friend of Mathilde Scholl, a significant personality in Rudolf Steiner's life. They were both part of the intimate esoteric circle which surrounded Dr. Steiner during the years 1904-14.

Gracia Ricardo took every opportunity to inquire about the spiritual realities of tone. When she asked Rudolf Steiner what the future held in store for song and for singers, he answered that singing must be freed from the physical mechanics of the "voice box" and awakened to the production and understanding of true tone, which is spiritual in nature.

Through many conversations with Rudolf Steiner, the many references to singing that she discovered in his writings, and from her own experiments, Gracia Ricardo developed a singing method based on the *word*. This method is distinctive because the singer does not begin with the usual vocal exercises. Instead, the student's attention is directed to speech. A word's initial consonant provides the sculptural form that holds the intoning vowels. The vowels and consonants become tone-creating vehicles in the element of air, and the voice is then released from its bodily prison.

A great change in Gracia Ricardo's life came about when she had to have an operation that resulted in the severing of the diaphragm muscles—she lost the breath control needed for concert singing. From then on, she put all the warm, generous vitality that had flowed into her musical career into furthering Rudolf Steiner's work and into her teaching. In this service, by means of her outgoing and organizational talent, she touched and stimulated various facets of anthroposophical work, as well as the course of many people's lives. Through her unique method, she enabled singers to rejuvenate their voices and produce a free, etheric tone. She was even able to bring about the total disappearance of nodules on the vocal cords, allowing many singers to return successfully to their careers.

Rudolf Steiner also entrusted her with the special task of introducing anthroposophical medicine and the Weleda remedies to North America. She was largely responsible for the immigration of two anthroposophical physicians, Christoph Linder in the 1920's and Siegfried Knauer twenty years later. Gracia Ricardo also helped introduce Weleda to England. An American physician, commenting on her promotional abilities, once remarked that "the lady could undoubtedly succeed in selling ice to Eskimos."

Eventually, a brownstone house in New York City, purchased through the generosity of Irene Brown, a pioneer American anthroposophist, served as a studio for Gracia Ricardo's singing activities. Some of her pupils were renowned artists, such as Elizabeth Rethberg, leading soprano of the Metropolitan Opera for many years; Berty Jenny and Erika Frauscher (both of whom sang successfully for many years in European theaters); and Marion Freschl, former head of the opera departments at both the Curtis Institute in Phildelphia and at the Juilliard School of Music in New York. Hilda Deighton and Gina Palermo, both prominent professional singers of their time, were also among her students.

This same brownstone provided storage for Weleda medicines, as well as space for the first classroom of the original Waldorf School in the United States. It also provided an office for Dr. Linder, the first anthroposophical doctor in America. Gracia Ricardo and Irene Brown also sponsored Lucy Neuscheller, the first eurythmist in this country. Thus Gracia Ricardo was "on the ground floor" of the pioneering effort to bring anthroposophical work to our western world.

Rudolf Grosse, a member of the Executive Committee (the Vorstand) and a former president of the General Anthroposophical Society in Dornach, Switzerland, said of the singer: "Gracia Ricardo was a significant individuality and was highly respected by Dr. Steiner. She was a very warm-hearted person, a *Weltmensch* (a citizen of the world). She would often invite me as a very young man for tea, and we would have many conversations about anthroposophy and the Anthroposophical Society."

During her later life, Gracia Ricardo divided her time between the Goetheanum in Dornach, Switzerland and America. When in Dornach, her devoted pupils Hilda Deighton, Gina Palermo, and I would often join her for considerable periods of continuing study.

She taught singing until she was eighty-four years old and at that time wrote: "I still have the great satisfaction of giving what I was privileged to have had accepted by Rudolf Steiner as one of the ways of training the voice through a method of interpreting the spiritual significance of the tone through its vehicle—the Word."

The following is one of her poems:

In every tone that through the lips doth flow
There lives the warmth which in the soul must grow.
Tone's mirrored hue will thus a picture be
Of inner life by ringing voice set free.

ADDENDUM:

An Acknowledgment

The 33rd anniversary of Gracia Ricardo's death prompts me all the more to get this book printed. Her significant contribution has been greatly enhanced during the intervening years.

She introduced me to anthroposophy, which proved a veritable lifesaver during my thorny destiny. It is out of my deep indebtedness to her that in my advanced years and declining health, I can summon up the forces to assemble these biographical sketches, many stemming from certain periods when destiny didn't permit me to be studying with Aunt Grace. So, therefore, I gratefully acknowledge the following:

Arvia Ege's editorial help in Aunt Grace's biography; Hilda Deighton and Gina Palermo's article in the 1981 Spring *Journal for Anthroposophy*; Hilda Deighton's book, *The Earliest Days of Anthroposophy in America*; Howland Vibber's "In Memoriam: Hilda Deighton" (in the *Anthroposophical Society Newsletter,* Summer 1976); Hilda Deighton's "In Memoriam: Gina Palermo" (in the *Anthroposophical Society Newsletter,* Summer 1963); *Newsletter* excerpts from papers of Aunt Grace's closest friend, Lucy Neuscheller, mother of Maria Renold, who sent them to me; Rudolf Grosse of the Vorstand of the General Anthroposophical Society in Dornach; Dr. Virginia Sease of the Vorstand of the General Anthroposophical Society, who graciously wrote the foreword to this book; and, of course, Hilda Deighton and Gina Palermo's patient and dedicated work of years in transcribing the substance of Gracia Ricardo's approach to singing. Because they were unable to finish the work, many sections remained incomplete and in need of revision.

Most of all, therefore, I must acknowledge Dina Soresi Winter's wholehearted recognition of Aunt Grace's singing method and my further developed technique, which resulted in her editing, revising (and adding to) this book which is published now in the hope that it will help other singers to experience the free tone.

In closing, many thanks go to Mark Finser. I never would have come through without his encouragement and pertinent suggestions and business and liaison expertise.

To all—heartfelt thanks and appreciation.

Theodora Richards,
December 1988

II

HILDA DEIGHTON

Hilda Deighton was born in Huntington, Indiana, on December 9, 1890, the youngest of nine children. Her father was a protestant pastor. Records of her family genealogy indicate that an ancestor, Sir Walter de Dyghton, was a Templar Knight who took charge of the Knights Templar Protectory at Temple Newsham, in Yorkshire, in 1181 A.D.

The impulse to sing came early in Hilda's life. She began her career in the northwest. From Seattle, Washington, she traveled to Chicago and Boston in search of a singing teacher. A Boston clergyman told her of Herbert Wilber Greene, an eminent tenor and teacher in New York City. While a pupil in his Conservatory in 1910, she met a circle of friends who formed the St. Mark's Study Group in Anthroposophy. Hilda Deighton was a member of this group, which was the first "official" Group of the Anthroposophical Society in America, and remained a member of it for the rest of her life.

During her career as a professional singer she sang for Protestant, Catholic, and Jewish congregations, and performed in opera. While on a trip to Italy in 1919 to gain additional experience in Italian opera, and to Dornach where she stayed for a time in order to take some singing lessons from Gracia Ricardo, whose devoted pupil she had become, she met Rudolf Steiner for the first time. The weekend she arrived Steiner was lecturing, giving the course that has been published in English as "The Mysteries of Light, Space and of the Earth." After hearing him, she wrote in her diary:

I went to hear him and this was the most important event in my life. After the lecture, Fraulein Scholl introduced me to him. I had never before stood in such a presence and was so overwhelmed I could never after quite remember exactly what he said to me at that first meeting.

Two things reigned supreme in the life of Hilda Deighton: her commitment to the spiritual approach to singing which she found through her work with Gracia Ricardo, and her love and devotion to anthroposophy. She served others through her art, which was further facilitated through the deep and lasting friendship she formed with Gina Palermo, whom she met at Herbert Wilber Greene's singing studio in New York City. Together they sang many concerts in the United States and abroad. Some of their most memorable performances were from the stage of the Goetheanum in Switzerland.

For many years Hilda Deighton led a chorus in Spring Valley,

New York, which performed every Christmas, at many summer conferences, and on other occasions. Her role as singing teacher was, according to one of her pupils (Howland Vibber), "surely her leading task during her lifetime. Her ability to convey to a pupil how to use the body as a musical instrument was something of a revelation for those who studied under her guidance." Hilda Deighton died at the Rudolf Steiner Fellowship Community in Spring Valley on March 20, 1976.

III

GINA PALERMO
Born November 15, 1901, Haverstraw, New York.
Died February 9, 1963, Spring Valley, New York.

Gina Palermo loved Albert Steffen's "Little Myth" which begins by describing a child standing near his father's coffin. The myth continues

At once the boy began to sing. "Be quiet," commanded his mother, "don't you see that your father is lying there?" At this, a man, who had been standing behind a pillar, appeared in a white garment, and said, "He will not awaken to life until his son comes and sings to him." "Oh," said the woman, "the boy is so small, he scarcely knows the scale." Encouraged by the stranger, the boy began to sing, "do-re-mi." Immediately a ladder of light ascended from the coffin and the dead man rose up and climbed, rung by rung, to heaven.

Gina appreciated this picture of the power of singing because she had a real grasp of *tone* in contrast to mere *sound* so prevalent today.

I like to recall the ways in which her beautiful singing helped the Anthroposophical Society—in Spring Valley, New York, and in Dornach, Switzerland. Coming to Spring Valley as early as 1942, she made sure we presented not just an ordinary program of solos and duets, but a really fine evening of music every summer at the Main Conference. In New York, we sang and collaborated with Hans Pusch and Paul Nordoff on many occasions in programs of speech and singing. During the war years, her concerts helped to raise a great deal of money for the Waldorf School in Stuttgart and for the Hoover Milk Fund. Often, when a friend had died, the gray bleakness of some obscure funeral parlor was suddenly, lovingly, filled with the sunshine of her high, radiant tone.

In the thirties, we made four trips to Dornach to study with Gracia Ricardo, whose method of tone production became our life interest. A few weeks before her death, Gina was still working on the book which we had been commissioned to write about these ideas of an etheric, body-free tone. In Dornach, we gave solo and duet recitals, singing works of Hindemith, Hans Gal, Bach, Handel, and Mozart. At the Goetheanum Gina also sang Jan Stuten's "Chinesische Lieder" with the Basel Symphony Orchestra. At this time the Basel *National Zeitung* wrote:

It is a sheer delight to hear in this warm pure soprano voice, the sparkling easy attack, the effortless blending of registers, and the gleaming top notes. It is also satisfying to marvel at the masterful schooling of this gorgeous gift. Here is the magic of a voice phenomenon, carefully fostered and scrupulously matured.

Gina proved tireless in her efforts to unearth Goethe songs from the Forty-Second Street Library. These were not merely settings of Goethe's poems by Schubert or Wolf, but the arrangements of his verses that were composed by his friends—

105

arrangements that Goethe often heard and loved to sing himself. We gave many varied programs featuring only the works of anthroposophical composers. I think we were unique in this. We sang the music of Paul Nordoff, Norman Vogel, John Schwabenland, and all the Dornach composers. The last concert Gina gave with me was at the Anthroposophical Society headquarters in New York City in November, 1961, rounding out the Centennial Year and consisting entirely of the compositions of musicians who are members of the Anthroposophical Society. Irene Laney was our accompanist.

Gina was led to anthroposophy by her longing to sing. She was offered lessons by her brother when in her early twenties, although her mother said, "Why waste money? She only has a low, husky voice." When she wrote to the Singing Teachers' Association, asking who was the finest teacher in New York, she was given the name of Herbert Wilber Greene at Carnegie Hall. Here the very first precious work of anthroposophy was being carried on. She found it and as I was teaching there, we met.

Gina had a gift for writing and lecturing. Her lecture on "Singing in the Past, Present and Future," given at the first of the Art Conferences organized by Richard Kroth in Spring Valley, has been printed in England. Her talk on "Goethe and Music," given in New York and published in the Anthroposophic News Sheet for April, 1962, has been put into Braille and is available at the Lighthouse for the Blind in New York.

In 1962, the year before she died, Gina was scheduled to give a talk at the Main Conference in Spring Valley on "Minstrelsy, Bards, Troubadours and Minnesingers." Being unable to leave her bed, she coached me carefully on how she wanted me to read it.

Above all, Gina Palermo was a servant of her art and of anthroposophy. One of her most important life deeds was her contribution to *Singing and the Etheric Tone*. She was working on the manuscript up to a few weeks before her death.

(Based on an account by Hilda Deighton)

IV

DINA SORESI WINTER

Dina Winter studied music at Mannes College of Music and Hunter College. She was a winner of the Blanche Thebom Scholarship Award, a national award for promising singers in the United States. This soon led to an additional award for study abroad, as a result of which she sang leading roles in major theaters in Italy and Germany. She now dedicates her time to teaching the Ricardo Method in the United States and Europe.

BIBLIOGRAPHY

Deighton, Hilda, *The Earliest Days of Anthroposophy in America*, privately printed.

Goethe, Johann Wolfgang, *Tonlehre.*

Greene, Herbert Wilber, *The Singer's Ladder.*

Greene, P., *Interpretation in Song.*

Lehmann, Lilli, *How to Sing*, Northbrook, Illinois: Whitehall Publishers, 1972.

Steffen, Albert, *Meetings with Rudolf Steiner* (translated by Rex Raab, Erna McArthur, Virginia Brett), Dornach, Switzerland: Verlag für Schöne Wissenschaft, 1961.

Steiner, Rudolf, and Steiner-von Sivers, Marie, *Poetry and the Art of Speech* (translated by Julia Wedgwood and Andrew Welburn), London: London School of Speech Formation, 1981.

Steiner, Rudolf, *Art as seen in the Light of Mystery Wisdom* (translated by Pauline Wehrle and Johanna Collis) London: Rudolf Steiner Press, 1984..

Light [First Scientific Lecture Course (*Light Course*)] Ten lectures given in Stuttgart, December 23, 1919 to January 3,1920 (translated by George Adams) Forest Row, East Sussex RH18 5JB, England: Steiner Schools Fellowship Publications, Michael Hall, 1987.

The Inner Nature of Music and the Experience of Tone (translated by Maria St. Goar), Hudson, New York: Anthropsophic Press, 1983.

"Die Völkerseelen und das Mysterium von Golgatha" ("Folk Souls and the Mystery of Golgotha"), Lecture, March 30, 1918: in *Erdensterben und Weltenleben. Anthroposophische Lebensgaben. Bewusstseinsnotwendigkeiten für Gegenwart und Zukunft* (GA181), Dornach, Switzerland: Rudolf Steiner Verlag, 1967.

RECOVERING THE SOURCES OF MEANING:
THE PATH OF ANTHROPOSOPHY

Anthroposophy is not just an abstract philosophy but a living spiritual path that reconnects human beings to the universe and to the sources of what it means to be human. Rudolf Steiner, who renewed this path of meaning in our time, saw four of his books as fundamental to the recovery of human dignity. Despite the many other books he wrote, and the more than 6,000 lectures he gave, Steiner returned again and again to these four basic books.

The Philosophy of Spiritual Activity

This fundamental work of philosophy demonstrates the fact of freedom. Read properly, the book leads the reader to experience the living thinking by which all human activity may be renewed.

Knowledge of the Higher Worlds and its Attainment

This fundamental guide to the anthroposophical path of knowledge. Steiner details the exercises and moral qualities to be cultivated on the path to conscious experience of super-sensible realities.

Theosophy

This work begins by describing the threefold nature of the human being. A profound discussion of reincarnation and karma follows, concluding with a description of the soul's journey through the supersensible regions after death.

An Outline of Occult Science

This masterwork places himanity at the heart of the vast, invisible processes of cosmic evolution. Descriptions of the different members of tthe human being, are followed by a profound investigation of cosmic evolution .

For prices and a catalogue of the more than 300 titles published and distributed by the Anthroposophic Press, please write to:

Anthroposophic Press
RR4, Box 94-A1
Hudson, NY 12534

518-851-2054